Shakespeare among Schoolchildren

Shakespeare among Schoolchildren

Approaches for the Secondary Classroom

Mary Ann Rygiel
Auburn High School, Alabama

National Council of Teachers of English
1111 Kenyon Road, Urbana, Illinois 61801

Manuscript Editor: Marya M. Ryan

Interior and Cover Designs: Doug Burnett

Cover Photo: James E. Corley

NCTE Stock Number 43814–3050

Library of Congress Cataloging-in-Publication Data

Rygiel, Mary Ann.
    Shakespeare among schoolchildren : approaches for the secondary classroom / Mary Ann Rygiel.
       p.   cm.
    Includes bibliographical references (p.   ).
    ISBN 0-8141-4381-4
    1. Shakespeare, William, 1564–1616—Study and teaching (Secondary)—United States. 2. Drama—Study and teaching (Secondary)—United States. 3. Drama in education—United States. I. National Council of Teachers of English. II. Title. III. Title: Shakespeare among school children.
PR2987.R9   1992
822.3′3—dc20
                                      92-6100
                                      CIP

I walk through the long schoolroom questioning;
A kind old nun in a white hood replies;
The children learn to cipher and to sing,
To study reading-books and history,
To cut and sew, be neat in everything
In the best modern way—the children's eyes
In momentary wonder stare upon
A sixty-year-old smiling public man.

—W. B. Yeats
"Among School Children"

Contents

Acknowledgments

Special thanks are owed to the following:

The National Endowment for the Humanities, for allowing me to do the research necessary to write this book by awarding me the NEH/Reader's Digest Teacher-Scholar award for Alabama for 1989–1990, and to Professor James Hammersmith, of Auburn University's English department, for being my mentor during that year.

The staff of the Ralph Brown Draughon Library at Auburn University, especially Glenn Anderson, for cheerful, courteous, patient help, and the staff of the Folger Library in Washington, D.C., for making my visit there a pleasure.

My friend Martha Solomon, professor of Speech Communication at the University of Maryland, for offering home and hospitality to me during my visit to the Folger, for urging me to write this book, and for offering a critique of the manuscript.

Family, including my husband Dennis and my sons Stephen and Robert, my brother Reverend Peter Heidenrich, O.P., and my sister Rose Bosau; my deceased parents Marshall and Eleanor Heidenrich; my in-laws, Robert and Clara Reitz; friends; teaching colleagues; and students past and present at Auburn High School are all owed debts which range from the intellectual to the motivational and spiritual and are too numerous to specify.

Finally, the fine staff at NCTE, especially Robert A. Heister, who oversaw editing and production, and Marya Ryan, the manuscript editor, who has been an advocate of clarity, consistency, logic, and readability and a vigilant eliminator of error. As we came closer to finishing, I began to feel that I was trapped in Zeno's paradox, i.e., able to cut distances in half but never able to quite cross the finish line. Any errors which do remain are mutant, stubborn strains of my own cultivation. Two of my students who loved *Dead Poets' Society* and its reference to *Midsummer Night's Dream* have reminded me of Puck's promise to amend.

1 Introduction

One aim of English teaching is to make connections between writers in their milieu and students (as readers, writers, actors) in theirs. Historical information contributes to our understanding of Shakespeare and our pleasure in him. The aim of this book is to make some connections for teachers between Shakespeare and his historical context on the one hand and secondary students on the other. Shakespeare is a writer whose work is the richer for being understood in context: he lived in a rhetorical age, before Puritan and scientific strictures on writing directed all writing toward the plain style. He faced the constraints other writers face from their own education and inherited native language and native theatrical traditions, as well as the challenges of the nuts and bolts of writing—rough drafts ("foul papers"), occasional stinging criticism from friends and consequent revision (see "Ben Jonson" in Campbell and Quinn, 1966), the need to skirt censors, the pressure of deadlines and interruptions, the desire to please an audience, the judicious and most effective use of sources, and, on occasion, having work stolen or marred by others.

The work directly on Shakespeare or in some way relevant to him could constitute a library, and in fact does—the fine 280,000 volume Folger Library in Washington, D.C. However, relatively little work has been done on Shakespeare the dramatist by secondary teachers for an audience of secondary teachers.

We secondary teachers need historical materials to help us place Shakespeare in his Renaissance context; we also need practical classroom follow-ups. Our student populations are more heterogeneous and less advanced on Piaget's formal reasoning scale than the college and university populations taught by the usual writers on Shakespeare. Sometimes the information that a scholar relegates to a footnote might actually be more interesting to a young student of Shakespeare than a dry, abstract, more seemingly relevant concept. I am thinking, for example, of the information Roland Mushat Frye provides in a footnote about fighting in or around churches in Elizabethan England, especially the reference to the pin stuck in Edy Alefounder during service. My ninth graders find this kind of information more interesting than discussions about the source of a monarch's power. If our students are more restless than older students, they are also often more honest (sometimes painfully so), sincere, open, affectionate, and more eager to learn and experiment than are older populations.

Our views of Shakespeare go hand in hand with our views of writing. In English classrooms today in America, many views of writing are held, some even alternately in the same room. Writing may be seen as an expression of the self or an expression of a unique vision which only the writing self has experienced and which it wishes to communicate to others. Writing may be seen as a statement of truth applicable in all times and for all cultures; such writing includes religious doctrines, philosophy, mathematical axioms and systems, poetic truths or "universals," and some moral law codes, such as Mosaic Law. Writing may be seen as instrumental, that is, not important in itself but in what it leads to, whether the result is a batch of fudge-nut brownies or improved driving skills. Writing may be seen as an act of interpretation by a community, such as a group of scientists classifying and describing the contents of plant or animal cells, or a group of feminists reading a play in a certain way. The extreme version of this view is to see writing as completely culturally determined. Regrettably, some others still occasionally see writing as a punishment to be inflicted on wayward students.

Shakespeare's writing has been seen in all these ways. Since the advent of the New Criticism in the English classroom, his work has been primarily viewed through the lens of the first two—as self-expression or as a statement of truth. The uniqueness of his insights and the unsurpassed nature of his writing have been stressed in English classrooms, but sometimes with deleterious effects. Students may be intimidated by a sacred-scripture approach to a writer who did not think of himself as a theologian but as a working dramatist. Much less often (until recent years) has Shakespeare been seen more instrumentally, i.e., as someone who wrote playscripts meant to be performed. Nor has he been seen as someone whom a class in one scheduled period of the school day might interpret differently than a class in another period. And seldom has he been seen in the secondary classroom as someone arising out of the context of the English Renaissance.

My first chapter presents an overview of some of the ways literary scholars and critics have approached Shakespeare. Each subsequent chapter is based on some aspect of Shakespearean scholarship and/or criticism. Each chapter includes classroom activities. My primary focus is on the four "school" tragedies most commonly studied in our high schools today—*Romeo and Juliet, Julius Caesar, Macbeth,* and *Hamlet*—although occasional references are made to other Shakespeare plays as well.

I begin here by stating my assumptions, arrived at inductively, about Shakespeare, drama, and students, and the relevance of Shakespeare and drama to students.

Shakespeare is mimetic and populist. His thoughts find expression in profound and memorable language, but he is not remote from human concerns. Rather, he wrote in the middle of them.

Drama engages the affections. This highly significant feature is seen in Hamlet's own reactions to the story unfolding before him, as when he exclaims "Poor Ghost!" or, at the end, "Wretched Queen." The presentational aspects of drama are important. The use of gestures, facial expressions, and varied voices can help drama come alive in our classrooms.

Students at all ability levels can and do enjoy Shakespeare. Moreover, students at all levels have insights into Shakespeare—whether it is into the no-turning-back, lifetime-of-happiness-in-two-days nature of the passionate young love in Romeo and Juliet, the fairy-tale quality of Friar Laurence's potion, Marc Antony's desire for revenge for his fallen friend, or the save-your-own-neck fleeing of the Senate after Caesar's murder—by which they can teach the teacher something new in a play. Students do read plays as interpretive communities, but my students see neither the nobility of Brutus nor the eventual treachery of Antony. All but the hams among my "regular" readers do not like long speeches.[1] Students will not always find greatness in the same places the teacher does, and they will laugh harder at the writer's slips (the discovery of Juliet's apparently cold body on the morning of her wedding to County Paris by Nurse and parents—all falling in deep "Oh!"s) and stylistic features (lots of lines of talk before dropping dead on stage). Students will ask many questions about Shakespeare's work and life. In fact, these questions formed the basis of this book. The students planted the seeds in my memory. I reap what they have sown, in hopes that others will come after, garnering ideas into their classrooms.

As teachers, we can build a repertoire of approaches to suit the variety of students we encounter in the classroom. The basis of these approaches is a recognition of the relevance of drama to our own lives. Students can be encouraged to give their personal responses to Shakespeare, not just read the plays as examination texts. Students can be encouraged to see how they appropriate the world of the theatre in their own lives. For example, they already have some awareness of varying audiences, and they often instinctively adjust their own language to those audiences. But they often enough do more than this, and even at an earlier age than they are aware of. My younger son, Robert, wrote me this note one day as a reminder of an errand I had promised to run for him: "Get Cubs team set '89 Upper Deck Say you are Mary Ann Rygiel spell last name Go at 12:00." This nineteen-word note includes dialogue, action, and stage directions. About the only thing missing is the theatre critic's review—and there are voices these days, such as George Steiner's, saying that this is exactly the part of the literary enterprise we don't need. Such scripting happens all the time, in a grisly way in the sensational Boston murders of wife and unborn child committed by Charles Stuart, or Romania's staging of the Ceausescu firing squad executions, and more humorously, in World Wrestling Federation threats and counterthreats, challenges and counterchallenges, issued by Hulk Hogan, who plans to leave wrestling for preaching, and Randy "Macho Man" Savage, who took a dizzyingly Macbeth-like descent into murkiness during his confederation with the fiend-like, sensational Sherry in the late 1980s. Students can be encouraged to do research in their own school libraries on such topical matters. Since such stories have a short but intense life in the media and popular culture, a number of articles accessible to high school students can be found in widely disseminated news magazines and other popular culture magazines. Such small-scale research can begin with a search of *The Reader's Guide to Periodical Literature*. The focus of the assignment can vary. One teacher's objective may be specifically to have students research contemporary, topical analogues to matters encountered in a contextualized study of Shakespeare, while another teacher's objective may be the broader one of requiring students to produce a documented essay (*not* a term paper) in which a point of view is established, a thesis maintained and supported by deployment of evidence, and a brief, correctly written bibliography (five items) appended.

The mystery of Shakespeare's plays—the mystery of genius focusing on what is essential and lasting in human nature and human experience—is that even in their Renaissance topicality, they remain relevant today. Besides what they say about love, devotion, ambition, cruelty, fear, courage, death, and the life of the spirit, their attention to such things as plague or exorcisms coincides with our own attention, sometimes in startling ways. Last May, my ninth-grade classes were studying *Romeo and Juliet* in Auburn, Alabama. We had scheduled a trip to the Alabama Shakespeare Festival. We almost had to cancel our trip. Just as we finished Act V with its news that Friar John was detained in a quarantined house in Verona, and thus unable to carry Friar Laurence's message to Romeo in Mantua, our Auburn community was threatened with quarantine because of an outbreak of measles on the university campus. This year, as I have been pondering *King Lear* and the source of the devils' names in a Tudor propaganda book about a series of countryside exorcisms conducted by Jesuits in the early 1580s, the Roman Catholic cardinal of New York City revealed that exorcisms had been conducted in his diocese because of a rise of satanism in the area. ABC News carried a feature story about the incident; reporter Jeff Greenblatt, while skeptical of medieval depictions of red-flannel devils, nonetheless noted the sure reality of evil as a force in the twentieth century.

The social and political contexts I present in the following chapters have been developed from my reading in works of history and biography, studies of the medieval and Elizabethan theatres, and literary critical studies, as well as my own inspection of various printed and manuscript works of the sixteenth century which yield insights into Shakespeare's plays. The activities I present will offer teachers a wide range of possibilities. Some come from suggestions in teaching journals; others come from my own classroom. They include large- and small-group discussion, journal and essay writing, ideas for classroom acting, bringing in guest speakers, and use of multiple media, as well as possibilities for nontraditional student engagement offered by such events as Renaissance fairs. If this mixture seems to assume a teacher who is a versatile jack-of-all-trades, I answer that teaching makes *Johannes factotums* of us all.

Note

1. Robert Weimann reports on a 1977 Berlin production of *Hamlet* in which an "impatient First Player . . . appeared almost bored by Prince Hamlet's advice" (1985, 290, *n.* 13). When I read this, I thought of my impatient Players, my students.

2 Literary Criticism, Shakespeare, and the Classroom

In this chapter I invite teachers to think about literary as well as scholarly approaches to Shakespeare for the purpose of examining their own philosophy of literature and its implications for their classroom practice. Some teachers who are invited to think broadly about any aspect of their philosophy of education may not want to. They have a negative emotional reaction to such an invitation based on prior associations with the question: possibly a college course they found too theoretical (all talk and no action), an essay on the topic they had to produce at their school system's central office when they were applying to teach in the system, or after-school or committee meetings they had to attend in order to formulate and explicitly state a philosophy.[1] Moreover, scrutiny of the school curriculum or of one's own views of the goals of education can be painful, carrying with it the possible suggestion that change is needed in thinking and in practice. Finally, some teachers will say, "I get along just fine without any theories. I only need skill pages and a copying machine." I don't think the members of this last group are my readers. I hope and trust they do not represent the majority in our profession.

But the others, the ones who are reluctant because of the connotations of words like "philosophy" and "theory," are my readers, I hope. These teachers may be new to teaching Shakespeare, or they may have been in the field awhile. They want to go beyond their current understanding of Shakespeare. They want to rejuvenate their own attitudes. As one classroom veteran of *Romeo and Juliet* said to me, "I am just tired of it. I'm tired of the Nurse and tired of them all."

Now, a ferment has been going on among secondary English teachers for the past two decades. English teachers have attended writing and dramatics workshops from the Bay Area to Bread Loaf; in the 1980s, they have attended National Endowment for the Humanities seminars for secondary teachers, more than ever before taken post-graduate work and earned higher degrees, been active in state and national councils and conferences. They write for professional education journals. Their knowledge of Shakespeare may be substantial and solid, yet they would like to deepen it.

An obvious solution is the abundance of printed material on all aspects of Shakespeare—from A to Z, from *Shakespeare against Apartheid* to Shakespeare and *Zodiake of Life*—available in a good university library. This cornucopia of material, cramming those bookshelves and tumbling daily from the presses of universities and scholarly journals, is daunting in itself, and recent literary criticism is especially so. Some teachers will say about the recent material, or even about all of this, "This does not have implications for the classroom."

I hope these hesitant pragmatists are my readers. Permit me to set up an analogy between your concerns and those of my own students. When I was showing a filmstrip on the Globe Theatre to a class of ninth graders, one boy asked, "What difference does it make that the stage was a rectangle?" Like fair and foul, simple and profound are sometimes not far apart. The physical aspects of the Elizabethan stage Shakespeare wrote for had enormous impact on his plays. Just to take one example, consider the punning commoners who speak almost immediately after the beginnings of *Romeo and Juliet* and *Julius Caesar.* This technique indicated to the groundlings, and to the seated "quality" as well, the need for attention to the dialogue in an open-air theatre. Or, to take another example, students readily enough learn the name of the trapdoor on the stage. Why not immediately associate the Hell with the special effects which issued forth from it?—the voice of the ghost of Hamlet's father commanding "Swear!" and the digging of Ophelia's grave or the witches' cauldron in *Macbeth.*

To the teachers who think like this perceptive student and who are therefore wondering, "Why does my private view of literature matter to my classroom?" the short answer is, "It matters enormously because it affects the structure of the individual class period, the structure of a unit of study, the types of assignments given, and the grading approach to those assignments."

I will give a brief survey of theory by way of answering a particular question. Along the way, I will suggest classroom implications and types of assignments suited to each approach's answer to the question. By the end of the survey, however, it should be clear that this approach of posing a question has been a device, a use of synecdoche to discuss the broader enterprise of the study of literature generally.

Survey of Scholarly and Literary Approaches

I will begin by asking you, "Who is standing behind the arras?" You might immediately respond by saying, "Polonius, of course," perhaps in a self-satisfied tone, or even in a derisive tone, indicating that you don't think much of me for asking such a simple question. Now, this rather simple six-word question has already evoked a complex set of reactions in you apart from your emotional response. For one, you might assume that the context in which the question is posed is *Hamlet* or a discussion of *Hamlet*. Two, you perhaps assume that I am looking for a one-word answer, an assumption based on previous school culture experiences, either tests or contest preparations which seek quick, one-word, univocal answers. It is disingenuous of me to pretend that the first assumption is false, for of course we are talking about *Hamlet*. However, I would like you to suspend assumption two, at least for the moment. Treat this question as a way of beginning to think about literary theory.

Various theories of meaning in literature are on the march today, competing not only for our attention but for our allegiance. I would like to introduce these theories, as well as some older ways of approaching literature, by the way in which each would answer the question I began with above.

New Criticism

One approach to this question about the arras is to study it as part of a pervasive pattern of images suggesting concealment, hiding, disguise, secrecy, spying. Maurice Charney notes in *Hamlet* the "large vocabulary of Machiavellian 'policy' words that give the play a distinctive atmosphere of anxiety and danger" (1969, 47). Charney studies other imagery patterns as well, assesses their relative importance, and relates all to a thematic reading stressing the "traditional warfare between good and evil" (316). In his chapter on Polonius, Charney sees him as a stage manager who specializes in concealments and who, "by some prophetic fatality of his university days" when he played the part of Caesar, is killed on stage by a Hamlet who earlier played Brutus (246).

Students can be faster than college professors in seeing through the gaseous haze that surrounds literary theory. After I introduced an advanced placement English class to some recent theory-oriented articles on *Hamlet* by university professors, one girl exclaimed, "That's not fair! Those people say they are going to write about *Hamlet*, but don't. And they get away with it. But when we get an assignment, we have to write about *Hamlet*." So, willy-nilly, theory is in the classroom too, even if it's crept in the back door and is hiding behind an invisible arras. The theory this girl was referring to, and which most of us in the classroom today operate on—the experienced among us at any rate—is New Criticism. Maurice Charney's work cited above is only in part New Critical, because he is also interested in the staging of Shakespeare's plays. However, he himself notes elsewhere: "Whatever our good intentions and whatever our stated commitment to theatrical values, we must still deal with Shakespeare primarily through the medium of reading" (1985, 891). New Critical purists stress the autonomy of the text as a pristine artifact of universal loveliness, a kind of Grecian urn which forever is, just is. New Criticism values the hunting through the text for imagery patterns, highly values paradox, ambiguity, and irony; and notes how the tensions created in the text are resolved in the ending. Steven Lynn states that the emphasis in the close reading of New Criticism is on *how,* not *what,* a work means, for the *what* must be experienced in the language of the work itself, ineffable in literary criticism (1990, 260).

Thus, in the New Critical classroom, each work is approached in isolation, in terms of the literary aspects noted above; moreover, the goal of any writing about a work is to evaluate the work. In the secondary classroom, this evaluative function of New Criticism is transmuted into the purpose of giving praise to the work, insofar as the student's own response is considered lesser in kind and quality than that of the anthology editor or the actual writer of the work being judged. A student writing about *Hamlet* might write about one or more of the imagery patterns Charney discusses in part one of *Style in Hamlet:* war, weapons, and explosives; secrecy and poison; corruption and its subcategories, animals, disease, food, gardens; limits, in terms of confinement, money, and numbers.

Authorial Intention

One theory for understanding a text focuses on the author. Hence, this theory would answer that it is the author who stands behind the arras. This theory, labeled the intentional fallacy by the New Critics, nonetheless is reasonable on commonsense grounds. Who would know better than an author what was intended by a particular text? However, the impossibility of questioning any dead author, and the elusiveness of Shakespeare's personality and intention in particular, are expressed in an interesting way by Henry James:

> The figured tapestry, the long arras that hides him, is always there, with its immensity of surface and its proportionate underside. May it not then be but a question, for the fullness of time, of the finer weapon, the sharper point, the stronger arm,

the more extended lunge? (qtd. in Campbell and Quinn 1966, 396)

This "revealing metaphor" (Campbell and Quinn 1966, 396), which paradoxically reveals and conceals at the same time, is particularly interesting in light of one theatre tradition which holds that Shakespeare was a prompter (Robert Speaight suggests he might have been a guider, i.e., a stage director [1973, 17]). It tantalizes us with the possibility that future discoveries could be made which would aid readers in understanding Shakespeare's intentions, even if the discoveries could not make such understandings undeniable. One need only look at the archaeological unearthing of the Rose and Globe foundations, with their evidence of hazelnut-munching audiences standing in the yard space of a round structure, or the work by Donald Foster on the dedication of the 1609 Quarto of Shakespeare's sonnets—a still unsolved riddle[2]—to know that we can come closer to obscured intentions.

An approach which focuses on the author of the work might result in a class on Poe, say, which would stress the link between the author's battle with drugs, alcohol, and the sufferings he endured in his love life and the strange morbidity of his stories and their neurasthenic narrators. Obviously this approach becomes more problematic in the case of a writer such as Shakespeare, to whom we have few references in other writing of the time. He is mentioned in Robert Greene, Frances Meeres, and the Cambridge plays *2 Parnassus* and *3 Parnassus*; there are references to him in the Master of Revels's payment books; and we have an authenticated bust, an authenticated portrait, signatures, legal papers, and church records for him (including baptism, wedding, and children's baptisms). There are quartos of about half his works, and the description "gentle" from Ben Jonson. None of this is the kind of personal, autobiographical detail we in the twentieth century relish. Hence, those who favor a biographical approach to the author must infer a biography, reading one from his plays. The result can be a statement such as Henry Wells's about the author's emotions:

> A world of oriental poetry goes down to defeat before a prosaic world of Roman discipline. The play shows Shakespere's (*sic*) dislike of the prosaic cunning of Augustus, and his bitter grief for those vices which made inevitable and just the tragedy of the Egyptians and their lord. ([1924] 1961, 223)

Or Muriel St. Clare Byrne's about the author's tastes:

> If asked what an Elizabethan household sent to the wash we might perhaps remember that Falstaff was rammed into the buck-basket with "foul shirts and smocks, socks, foul stockings, greasy

napkins" and carried to the laundress in Datchet-mead; but if we have ever thought about his description of these "stinking clothes" and their greasiness we are more likely to have related it to Shakespeare's acute personal dislike of foul smells and grease. (1966, 203)

Or the statement by the Anglican bishop Robert E. Terwilliger that Shakespeare was one of their "greatest theologians" (1981, 69).

Though these inferred biographical snatches may seem quaint and fanciful to us, one observation struck me as having great relevance and power. The Russian film director Grigori Kozintsev scornfully rejected the "full-length marble gentleman" in Westminster Abbey depicting Shakespeare in lace-cuffed clothes, with his elbow resting on deluxe editions, pillow at hand. This view was inconsistent with Kozintsev's concept of a man of the theater who worked for his daily bread (1966, 16). Following up on this discussion, students can study various artistic representations of Shakespeare and give their reasons for choosing one as most accurate. The most familiar portraits are the Chandos and the Droeshout engraving (both are reproduced in Campbell and Quinn 1966, 654–55). Older students might like to study the history of the portraits; they can begin with the article in Campbell and Quinn's *Reader's Encyclopedia* entitled "Portraits of Shakespeare."

The Author's Theatrical Contexts

Another approach to understanding a text recognizes that the text of, say, *Hamlet*, is in fact a play, and consequently this approach focuses on the stage in its historical context. By this theory, what might be said to be standing behind the arras is the traveling pageant wagons or the market booth stage of the popular medieval outdoor theatre. C. Walter Hodges and Robert Weimann, for example, have written on theatre history lying behind and surrounding Shakespeare's own theatre. This approach also focuses on the nature of the Globe Theatre props. Hence, the theater historian's answer about what stands behind the arras is possibly the artisan fashioner, the individual painter who painted the cloth so as to resemble a woolen tapestry wall hanging in one of the great houses in Elizabethan England. Such an approach would also focus on the use and location of the arras cloth on the stage itself (Hodges 1973, 41), including the observation that black hangings on stage designated a tragedy to the audience.

By extension, this theory looks at Continental analogues. In *The Globe Restored*, Hodges includes a plate (no. 26) of a Rederyker Theatre dumb show, The Tarquin Stage, Amsterdam, 1609. This plate shows an eavesdropper behind the arras in a *tableau vivant* depiction of the expulsion of the Tarquins from Rome. The eavesdropper overhears the plotting of the sons of Brutus with Tarquin and Sextus. Work later than Hodges's concludes that there was no influence from the *Rederijkers'* (Dutch rhetoricians') theatre on the Elizabethan theatre (Hummelen 1979, 164–89), but to know this takes us from the realm of speculative influence study to the realm of cultural anthropology, and it takes us to a conclusion.

Theatre historian Bernard Beckerman discusses Polonius's concealment as an "observation scene," an Elizabethan theatrical convention "closely allied to the aside in structure" (1962, 192). The location of Polonius in III.iv, Beckerman points out, is behind a hanging curtain concealing an enclosure. The approach Beckerman represents would look at the native literary context, both dramatic and otherwise, to learn about the Shakespearean intention. Such work might begin, as T. C. Baldwin's definitive study did, in a study of the aims and methods of the Elizabethan grammar schools; such work might focus on the two notable universities of the time, Oxford and Cambridge, as did Craig Thompson's. Such work would go on to study the ultimate flowering of the schools in the plays, poetry, and prose of the time. But any such attempt always faces the recognition that the grammar-school-educated Shakespeare and the bricklayer's son Ben Jonson exceeded the university wits. And work such as Edwin H. Miller's *The Professional Writer in Elizabethan England* frankly confronts the thorn of poverty which continually pricked most of the nondramatic writers in Elizabethan England.

Studies which focus on literary context might, like Geoffrey Bullough's, locate Thomas Kyd's *Spanish Tragedy* behind Shakespeare's arras, specifically listing twenty parallels between the two works (1973, 16–17). Bullough also focuses on the antecedent to both Kyd and Shakespeare, Saxo Grammaticus's *Historiae Danicae*, and François de Belleforest's translation of this work. In Book III of *Historiae Danicae*, Amleth is shut up with his mother but suspects the usurper Feng's cunning; Feng indeed had concealed a willing counselor in the *stramentum* (straw, straw mattress) (Bullough 1973, 65).

Teachers who are interested in medieval stage elements in Shakespeare, and more broadly in theatre history, have wonderful opportunities for student involvement. Teachers might follow up on the implications of Robert Weimann's bold view of *Hamlet* as a development of the medieval vice character in the role of "director and master of ceremonies theatrical" (1985, 285); lecture on the aspects of *de casibus* tragedy in the play,[3] with the concomitant idea of the clown/jester figure in the play in the persons of the gravediggers; or talk about how the wheel of fortune theme and the *ubi sunt* themes of medieval thought[4] come together powerfully in the gravediggers' scene.

Student assignments can include the enacting of medieval drama from the mystery and morality plays. They can also include the use of stage models of the Globe Theatre. Hodges has detailed sketches of his reconstruction in *The Globe Restored*. For students who are technically minded and/or good in physics, John Ronayne's article on decorative and mechanical effects includes fascinating material on such topics as lever-operated cloud thrones and the making of paints and brushes for various painted effects, such as the Heavens. Students who are crafts oriented often enjoy three-dimensional projects. For example, a study of chivalry in the medieval period can call forth beautiful shields made with construction paper or even highly figured wallpaper. This heraldic approach can work for the Renaissance, too. Students can begin with Shakespeare's own coat of arms (with its motto "Not without right") and Ben Jonson's parody ("Not without mustard") and develop their own. To return to our focus on the physical appearance of the theatre, students can make small models of the medieval booth stage theatres and script plays for their own hand puppets. Also, of course, they can try some of the decorative effects used in the Globe Theatre and described in Ronayne. Also, teachers can use the pictures of Shakespeare's actors available to us—such as those of Richard Burbage, Will Kempe, Robert Armin, and John Lowin (reproduced in Frye 1967, plate nos. 60–63)—in a guided discovery procedure about these actors' known parts, skills, and contributions to the Elizabethan stage.

Teachers who are interested in Shakespeare's native educational and literary context have a built-in motivation for taking a class to the library. Groups of students can locate and perform scenes from Marlowe, Ben Jonson, and Webster. Individuals can research minor writers noted in Miller's book on the professional writer in the Elizabethan period. The list includes, but is not restricted to, Robert Greene, Barnaby Rich, Thomas Nashe, Gabriel Harvey, George Peele, Anthony Munday, and John Marston. Many amusing parallels can be found between writers then and now—lack of appreciation and understanding on the part of their audience being the key similarity. Students can list others, focusing on the tricks of writers. I list them here for the benefit of teachers.

1. "Falconer" dedications.[5] The seventeenth-century writer Thomas Jordan carried a hand press with him on his rounds

to prospective patrons (Miller 1959, 122). How many students have written the same paper for more than one teacher?

2. Effusive flattery of patrons, sometimes followed by denunciations of patrons by disgruntled writers (99, 132). Don't students refer to the former technique as "buttering up" the teacher?

3. The hope that the patron's name would endorse the writing to the buying public (130). Aren't ads today which use star endorsements, such as Michael Jordan's, an obvious lure to buyers?

4. Brief tracts, entertaining "popular" works, repetitious plain style (208–10). Isn't this what we call "filler" today?

5. Profiteering from pain, such as rushing to write an epitaph of a dead noble (117–18). Doesn't this resemble today's sometimes ghoulish press?

6. Plagiarism (210). In his discussion, Miller makes clear that the best writers did not plagiarize, but others did so, including one Nixon, "who composed his books with scissors and paste" (210).

Students can also enact work by Thomas Kyd, specifically his *Spanish Tragedy,* and try to identify some of the parallels between Kyd's work and *Hamlet.*

Textual Editing

A technical and exacting method of study details manuscript and printing history, comparing quarto and folio copies in attempting to determine exact texts. In the Pelican Shakespeare text[6] of *Hamlet,* for example, the *Hamlet* editor, Willard Farnham, has supplied in brackets both additions to the stage directions found in the "good" quarto of 1604–1605 (Q2) and also the act and scene division itself. In this sense, then, Willard Farnham is behind the direction, "Polonius hides behind the arras," as well as the demarcation of the scene as III.iv (1969, 932, 957). An editor supplying a school edition might note the origin of the word "arras" in Norman French as well as the fame of the northern French city of Arras based on its fifteenth-century tapestries.

Teachers who somehow fancy an interest in textual editing need to begin with the services of an expert. A classroom lecture by a textual editor describing the profession in all its tedium and rewards is sure to be eye-opening to both teacher and students. For example, James Hammersmith has demonstrated that a textual editor needs to be able to duplicate English secretary hand in order to speculate about the range of readings an Elizabethan or Jacobean printer could have given a particular handwritten word when setting type in the printshop. This topic, technical as it is, allows for interesting student assignments as follow-ups.

   1. Students can simulate a printer in Jaggard's printshop by transposing a line of type from their text of Shakespeare onto a sheet of paper simply by copying the line by hand and comparing their results with the text and with classmates' versions.[7] (One must recognize, of course, that Jaggard's printers did not work from typescript unless they were printing from a quarto.) Because printers liked to carry lines in their head as they did their work, students will be interested to compare their results with the printed text and with each other's results to see what mistakes occur.

   2. Students will also be simulating printers from the time of the First Folio if they make an emendation to a line which they think is in error. For example, when Gertrude says to Hamlet in III.iv, "And there I see such black and grainèd spots" (Farnham 1969, 958), this is the 1623 Folio reading. The "good" quarto of 1604–1605 (Q2) uses the word "greeued." Brave students can edit a few lines of text where disagreement exists between one or more quartos and the First Folio; then they can attempt to list their principles of emendation. For example, are their emendations aimed at the contemporary adult reader, the high school reader, or the scholar? The Pelican *Hamlet* furnishes more than enough matter to worry over for a budding editor.

   3. Where no quartos preceded the 1623 Folio, as in the case of *Julius Caesar*, there is still an editorial question to ponder, one to which students can address themselves most feelingly—the question of character names. The most extreme student response to speech prefixes[8] in plays I have ever heard came from a boy who said he read *no* speech prefixes in his first reading, just reading text continuously. Other students who do bother to consult the speech prefixes are puzzled by alternate names for one character, but they do learn to adjust, though at differing rates. Stanley Wells identifies Latin forms, Italianate colloquial variants of the Latin name forms, and English name forms in *Julius Caesar* and concludes that in this play the "variation appears to reflect Shakespeare's frequent indifference to the form used" (1984, 48). However, rather than regularize Latin and Italian variants to Latin only, as most editors have done, Wells prefers to retain the Folio variants. Students may approach this editorial crux with relish and volubility. Moreover, they would learn lessons in both metrics and formal versus colloquial style in studying Caesar's use of the name Antonius and Brutus's use of the name Antony in I.ii.

   4. Students can supply stage directions for a scene. Wells's discussion of this topic is readable and easy to follow. Of special interest to a teacher and class are his comments on John Dover Wilson's stage directions as being novelistic rather than dramatic in character. Here is an example of Wilson's directions from *Julius Caesar:*

> Caesar rises, and struggles to escape; the conspirators close in upon him near Pompey's statue, and hack eagerly at him; he stands awhile at bay, until, seeing Brutus about to strike also, he covers his face. (qtd. in S. Wells 1984, 67)

5. Students—and teachers—who have wondered what is meant by the mysterious words "folio" and "quarto" are urged to try the folding directions given in George Williams's book *The Craft of Printing:*

> If readers wish to see how this works, they may take a sheet of paper, fold it once in a fold parallel to the short side, fold it a second time in a fold parallel to the (new) short side. They will then have a little quarto sheet. If they number the pages, from front to back 1 through 8, and then unfold the paper, they will see how the pages are disposed on each side (in each forme). They will notice also that two of the pages on each side are "upside down" and though two pages numbered consecutively may be back to back or side by side when the sheet is folded, those same two may be seemingly unconnected when the sheet is unfolded. The little sheet of paper thus marked will represent an actual *sheet* after it has been printed. To find the imposition of the *type* on the imposing stone, readers should place the same paper, now unfolded, over a new piece of paper the same size; then they should copy the numbers from each "page" on one side onto the new paper in the same order and position. The new paper will then represent the arrangement of the actual type of a single forme ready to receive the sheet to be printed. To secure the imposition of the other forme, they should turn the folded paper over, place it on another piece of paper, and repeat the process. (1985, 58)

Perhaps more than any number of descriptive words, these instrumental directions make clear what is meant by a quarto.

6. The teacher can issue copies of "To the great Variety of Readers" in an old spelling version; as a whole-class activity, with the teacher at the overhead projector, the class can modernize this Folio introduction in spelling and style, and in the process achieve class consensus on principles of emendation.

The Author's Social and Political Context

Once we leave approaches which focus either on the author or the author's literary context, we have crossed the border into different theoretical territory. Although we are still in the same time period, the Elizabethan, we now look at the sociopolitical context of the play. Instances of spying at court are almost too numerous to mention. I will refer to several involving royalty itself, as well as mention in passing that the Lisle letters, covering the period 1533–1540, clearly document the presence of "fee'd men" or "privy friends" in other people's households (Byrne 1981, xiii), thus also explaining a line in *Macbeth:*

> There's not a one of them but in his house
> I keep a servant fee'd.
>
> (III. iv. 131–32)

Elizabethan observer John Foxe reported the hidden presence of King Philip "behind a cloth, and not seen" (qtd. in J. Levine 1969, 17) at the meeting between Queen Mary Tudor and Elizabeth, when the imprisoned Princess Elizabeth was brought to Queen Mary from her confinement at Woodstock. That royalty found such hidden placements useful is evidenced again and again. Over twenty years later, when the Duke of Alençon renewed his suit to then Queen Elizabeth in 1579, at a time when the Privy Council, especially Lord Burghley, argued against this suit and two of the Queen's ladies were arrested for even discussing the matter, court members were forced to "shut their eyes" to the progress of the suit. At a grand ball where the Queen was reportedly unusually animated, Alençon was "placed behind a hanging" and the Queen made "signals to him" (J. Levine 1969, 109). Toward the end of her life, Elizabeth displayed a strangely Hamlet-like response to the arras in her privy chamber. Her godson, Sir John Harington, described her behavior after the Essex rebellion in this contemporaneous syntax:

> She . . . stamps with her feet at ill news, and thrusts her rusty
> sword at times into the arras in great rage. The dangers are over,
> yet she always keeps a sword by her table. (qtd. in Creighton
> 1893, 236)

Finally, from a time a little later than the earliest performance and quarto publications of *Hamlet*, we find yet another story, this time from the court of James, that suggests that intrigue and hiding were well known to royalty. For the deliberations of his second Parliament in 1614, James hid the Spanish Ambassador Sarmiento, Count Gondamar, "behind the silk curtain with holes in it" to hear deliberations (Fraser 1975a, 155).

Historical events with a different sort of relevance to the play can be found as well. New historicists ransack historical documents to locate specific historical events lurking behind the surface of an entire play. Annabel Patterson, for example, locates two historical events behind the arras of the play *Hamlet:* (1) the fiasco of the Earl of Essex's mission in Ireland in 1599, his stormy confrontation with the Queen, his eventual uprising and execution in 1601, and the subsequent disappointment felt by his supporters; and (2) the competition given the adult theatres by the boy actors of St. Paul's. These events precede and surround Shakespeare's 1601 *Hamlet* (1988, 55–61). The student of sources, Geoffrey Bullough, discusses the topicality of a *Hamlet* on the boards around 1587–1589, in which Bullough finds possible reference either to Elizabeth's murder of Mary, Queen of Scots, in 1587 and the need for Mary's son James to avenge her execution, or, more likely, a reference to the murder in 1567 of James's father, Lord Darnley, and the unseemly haste of Mary's marriage to Lord Bothwell (1973, 18–20). In other ways, individual figures within the play are located in the historical time period. Elizabeth's Lord Treasurer, William Cecil, Lord Burghley, is thought by some to be the model for Polonius (Campbell and Quinn 1966, 90). Others find in the conversation between Hamlet and his mother in III.iv a basis in the relationship between Mary, Queen of Scots, and the Earl of Bothwell, alluded to above in Bullough's assumption of this episode's topicality and relevance to earlier *Hamlet*s.

Teachers who are interested in the interlocking political, religious, social, and intellectual contexts of Shakespeare's plays have a rich wealth of materials to draw on, including the letters by the professional letter writer of the time, John Chamberlain (see Thomson 1965); the diary of the law student, John Manningham (see Sorlien 1976); as well as many histories and biographies of figures of the period. Those who want to somehow relive the time from 1591 to 1603 can read G. B. Harrison's year-by-year reconstruction of this period. Several recurrent themes emerge: the activities and the discontent of the Earl of Essex, the courageous missionary activity and controversies involving the English Jesuits, and the fear of a re-outfitting of the Spanish Armada. In his seminal work *The Crisis of the Aristocracy,* Lawrence Stone makes it clear that positions available at court to absorb the energies, loyalty, and commitment of ambitious nobles did not keep pace with the sheer numbers of such nobles (1967, 213–15). As a point of comparison, students can list positions in school, a microcosm of society, which give status, both those that give status to teachers and those that give status to students. Students who are interested in economics can study the chart (included in this chapter) of sample money values from the Elizabethan/Jacobean period and locate other historical money values

Elizabethan Extravagance and Economy

Item	Cost (in English pounds)	Year	Special notes	Source
country manors land-based receipts, including rent	100– over 10,000	1602		St. 70*
	1,630	1602	"Mean net income of a peer."	St. 68
construction of Hatfield House	40,000	1608–1612	Belonged to the Earl of Salisbury.	St. 254
London life:				
Elizabeth's coronation	16,741, 19 shillings, 8¾ pence	1558		Sm. 101
Elizabeth's annual household costs	40,027		Less than another royal Tudor family's would have been—Elizabeth was childless, single, and more frugal than her father.	Sm. 87
Elizabeth's administration costs annually, solely for fees and pensions	30,000			St. 197
marriage of Lord Burghley's daughter	629	1582		St. 256
titled gentleman's clothing annually	1,000	late 1590s	Titled men were expected to dress lavishly.	St. 258
courtier's annual costs	1,000		Minimum.	St. 208
courtier's annual costs, if officeholder	3,000			St. 208
exceptional courtiers' annual costs	5,000–10,000		The Earl of Essex, for example.	St. 208
annual worth of one highly placed courtier	3,500		This figure shows Walter Raleigh's income.	Sm. 94
Elizabeth's ten-day visit to Burghley's country house	900	1591	The less privileged could not afford a visit.	St. 209

Continued

Item	Cost (in English pounds)	Year	Special notes	Source
administrative salaries annually:				
Lord Treasurer	336	1608–1612	Actually worth £4,000, counting legal and illegal opportunities for income beyond the official fee.	St. 192
Mastership of Court of Wards (placed and handled the money for well-to-do minors)	133	1608–1612	Actually worth £3,000 (see previous note).	St. 192
Sweet Wine Farm annual lease (tax monopoly granted private individual—there were many)	2,500		Essex rebelled after Queen refused renewal in 1600.	St. 201
war costs to gov't:				
Dutch front	1.4 million	1585–1596		Sm. 202
Armada year	273,000	1588		Sm. 202
privately owned ship: 400 ton	1,500	1588	This figure shows the cost of the galleon Leicester.	St. 174
purchase of titles:				
baronet	1,095	1611		St. 44
peer	2,900	1605	£2,000 outright, plus expenses.	St. 51
bribery	wide variation		One noble allowed Queen to win £40 from him monthly at dice.	St. 260
gambling	wide variation		In 1603, Robert Cecil lost £800 in one night.	St. 260
"favors" of lady at court	300		Amount spent by Robert Leicester.	Sm. 123
Alençon's compensation	10,000 + handkerchief		Duke's compensation from Queen for his unsuccessful suit to her in prolonged courtship.	Sm. 182
writers and other lesser mortals:				
cost of travel abroad	80	1580s	Gentleman could manage on this annually.	St. 317

ordinary life in London, annually	40			Mi. 167
schoolmaster's annual salary	20			Sc. 212
Shakespeare's estimated annual income for fifteen years	200–233		Shakespeare's multiple roles as playwright, actor, and sharer in the company gave him a larger income; amateur playwrights not attached to a company made less.	Sc. 212
New Place (Shakespeare's country home)	60	1597		Sc. 234
writer's pensions: Ben Jonson	66	1611		Mi. 123
Edmund Spenser	50			Mi. 123
cost of books	2 or 3 sheets a penny			Mi. 162
fees given to writers by patrons for dedications	1		An average per title.	Mi. 126
cost Henslowe paid dramatists	6			Mi. 158
fine to printer without license:				Po. 21
ballad	4 pence			
book	12 pence			
Pepper, Politics, and Profit— a spicy mix:				
one pound of pepper	40 pence ($1.00)	1599	Price increases led to East India Company and onward to British Indian Empire.	Ta. 240
3,000 tons of spices	91,041 ($227,603) 789,168 ($1,972,920)	1621	Bought in Indies, sold in Aleppo.**	Ta. 236

* St. = Stone 1967; Sm. = Smith 1975; Mi. = Miller 1959; Sc. = Schoenbaum 1977; Po. = Pollard 1937; Ta. = Tannahill 1973. Abbreviations are followed by page numbers.

** Located in modern day Syria, Aleppo lies at the eastern end of the Mediterranean. It was a trading center for the overland spice route; it is mentioned as a foreign port by one of the witches in *Macbeth* and its centrality as a point of mingling for merchants—Mongols, Ottoman Turks, and Venetians—is alluded to by Othello in his final lines.

of their own. They can draw conclusions from this data and construct their own chart of analogous contemporary data. Students who are interested in religious topics and likely to be open-minded about the plight of both Catholics and Puritans in the forced Anglican settlement may want to write a story or play about the very dramatic escape of the Jesuit John Gerard from the Tower of London in 1597. Source materials include Christopher Hibbert's book *Tower of London* as well as John Gerard's own autobiography. The maps and pictures in Hibbert's book can be used as devices to stimulate thought as well as materials to guarantee some authenticity of account. Alternatively, students may want to write about the departure from England of the Puritans destined for the New World in the early seventeenth century. Many students seem to enjoy maps. The map of the course of the ill-fated Armada in Colin Martin and Geoffrey Parker's *The Spanish Armada* (1988, inside cover) might lead to excellent stories about the actual battles between the English sea dogs and the Spanish; other stories could focus on the disastrous outcomes for so many Armada vessels as they wrecked all along the western coast of Ireland on their circuitous route homeward. Students interested in early weapons and ships will find plenty to stimulate their imaginations in Martin and Parker's book. Students who do not wish to voyage as far afield as the New World or the western coast of Ireland can study the map of London's theatres and compose stories set in the London of Shakespeare's time. They could, perhaps, depict people departing from the steps at Blackfriars and gliding across the Thames for an afternoon at the Globe.

Recent Literary Theory

In our whirlwind tour of the territories of theory, whose armies of literary critics are on the march to extend their territory and claim our allegiance, we are coming to our final territory, which is at best a loosely unified group of republics. Reminding ourselves of our initial question, "Who is behind the arras?" let us turn to Johannis de Witt's sketch of the Swan playhouse (reproduced in Burgess 1970, 154). Above the stage, whose face is marked *mimorum aedes*[9] and on which three characters are playing, are people grouped by ones and twos in stage boxes. It has been variously debated that de Witt sketched a practice of a performance, in which case it is said that the individuals are actors waiting for their cues, or that these are wealthy spectators seated in an audience which is simply not fully depicted (Gurr 1987, 21). In this case, either the actors or the audience itself is behind the place where the arras would be.

Criticism concerned with the play beyond its original history may focus on productions or on audience reaction, including one's own reaction either to the printed text or to an enacted performance. Feminist Elaine Showalter, for example, is concerned to show how Ophelia has been presented on stage from 1601 to the present. In addition, Showalter is interested in how theatrical presentations interact with and alter other cultural phenomena. She describes the practice of Victorian psychologists of posing—or staging—madwomen in Ophelia-like clothing and props for the benefit of photographers, writers, and other observers (1985, 85–87).

Deconstructionist critic Terence Hawkes gives his own response to the play in "Telmah" (*Hamlet* spelled backwards). Taking a stance which notoriously refuses to be systematic, Hawkes purports to show in a circuitous way that *Hamlet* is nonlinear, folding back on itself. Hawkes asserts that Hamlet cannot trust the ghost of his father because King Claudius does not react to the dumb show. Hence, somewhere between III.iii and III.iv, *Hamlet* becomes *Telmah*. In the remainder of his essay, Hawkes focuses on the work of the politically conservative Shakespeare scholar and textual editor, John Dover Wilson, including Wilson's role in drafting the Newbolt Report, an influential document on English education issued by an education committee formed in May 1919. The report stressed the cultural unity among English economic and social classes which could be encouraged by the study of English literature. Hawkes feels that a Eurocentric view of literature cannot allow the coexistence of *Hamlet*, a play with a truth-telling ghost, and *Telmah*, a play in which doubt arises about the ghost's veracity. In a display of virtuoso writing, Hawkes concludes his essay with a verbal improvisation on American jazz and the literal translation of the name of Fortinbras, Hamlet's successor as king of Denmark, into Louis Armstrong (1985, 317–31). By now, we have come pretty far from our starting point, we are perilously close to psychoanalyst Jacques Lacan's Gallicism that the child is an "hommelette" (qtd. in Nuttall 1983, 29), and we are close to scrambling Hamlet into an omelet. However, Hawkes's discussion and point of view are in fact relevant to the current cultural debate in the United States over the social cement of a commonly possessed literary culture and historical awareness.

Nevertheless, let us return to our opening question. If you answered "Polonius," you were not wrong. Your answer was based on some assumptions. I specified two immediately. I will now specify another. Because you answered a question which you assumed to be based on play plotting, you answered within an Aristotelian context.

Aristotle, after all, was the literary critic who emphasized plotting, and moreover, plotting based on mimetic fidelity. Hence, I think our earliest literary critic would be pleased to see the efforts made by so many of our latest literary critics to contextualize Shakespeare, to show how his play action is a just imitation of life. Attempts to historicize Shakespearean drama appeal to our more advanced students. Also, such students might be glad to know they are in such good literary company. Aristotle might not be pleased with all the varieties of contemporary criticism, including certain varieties of reader-response criticism, since some seem to work to unravel the skein of theory he knit from the wool of Greek goats and their herders' songs. I speak of the patented, politically packaged responses which tend to be dogmatic: their unfurled banners are emblazoned with easily recognized, if not always intelligible, signs. In fact, the critic Annabel Patterson has issued a plea to such contentious critics to stop stabbing each other behind the arras (1988, 65).

Teachers who are interested in some of the more recent developments in literary criticism also have activities available for their classrooms. First, feminist criticism. Steven Lynn introduces the method of feminist reading as follows: "Part of its appeal, I suppose, is its simplicity, at least on the surface: to practice feminist criticism, one need only read as a woman. Such a procedure quickly turns out to have a profound effect on the reader and the text—an effect that hardly can avoid being political" (1990, 268). Students who have an interest in this topic might be interested in reading about the nineteenth-century American actress Charlotte Cushman, who played Romeo to her sister's Juliet, Hamlet, and Cardinal Wolsey in addition to a number of female roles. They might also be interested in looking into what was evidently a nineteenth-century rage for female Hamlets (see Winter [1911] 1969, 427–42). This topic can potentially generate fruitful discussion and/or performance. An example of a feminist reading which could generate class discussion is Carolyn Heilbrun's article, "The Character of Hamlet's Mother." A group of English teachers in a Shakespeare workshop I presented were most amused to consider Gertrude as a woman too old at age forty-five to be sexually attractive, if viewed as some English Shakespeare critics have viewed her. Second, teachers who are interested in deconstruction can get an orientation to the topic in the NCTE publication by Sharon Crowley, *A Teacher's Introduction to Deconstruction* (1989). This theory, though popular at the university level, has little practical applicability at the secondary school level. Hence, I have no suggestions to make other than the market cry, "caveat emptor" ("let the buyer beware").

Finally, reader-response criticism: Lynn briefly explains this theory as building a reading from the student reader's subjective response. This theory can be extremely productive in the classroom. I present the following seven topics as writing assignments. The teacher who wishes to use any of these can modify them for whole-class oral discussion, small-group discussion, or conferring with individual students, depending on the size, ability, interests, and cohesiveness of the class.

1. Picture yourself as a groundling watching a Shakespearean play. What features in the play particularly appeal to you? Also, how do you act during the play? Do your actions affect the performance?

2. Picture yourself as a character in the play. Create stage directions (including movement and facial expressions) for your character in a particular scene or act. Present this scene or act to the class.

3. Use the following poem by Zbigniew Herbert, "Elegy of Fortinbras," as a model. Write an elegy for another important but little-represented character in a Shakespeare play. Alternatively, read the poem "Purgatory" by Maxine Kumin on what might have happened to Romeo and Juliet in a happier ending. Write a happier, realistic ending for *Hamlet*.

Elegy of Fortinbras*

Now you have peace Hamlet you accomplished what you had
   to
and you have peace The rest is not silence but belongs to me
you chose the easier part an elegant thrust
But what is heroic death compared to eternal watching
with a cold apple in one's hand on a narrow chair
with a view on the ant-hill and the clock's dial

Adieu Prince I have tasks a sewer project
and a decree on prostitutes and beggars
I must also elaborate a better system of prisons
since as you justly said Denmark is a prison
I go to my own affairs This night was born
a star named Hamlet We shall never meet
what I will leave will not deserve tragedy

---

* "Elegy for Fortinbras" by Zbigniew Herbert, translated by Czeslaw Milosz. From *Encounter*, August 1961. Copyright © 1961 by Encounter, Ltd.

It is not for us to greet each other not bid farewell
and that water these words what can they do What can they do
    Prince

                    —Zbigniew Herbert, translated by Czeslaw Milosz

Purgatory**

And suppose the darlings get to Mantua,
suppose they cheat the crypt, what next? Begin
with him, unshaven. Though not, I grant you, a
displeasing cockerel, there's egg yolk on his chin.
His seedy robe's aflap, he's got the rheum.
Poor dear, the cooking lard has smoked her eye.
Another Montague is in the womb
although the first babe's bottom's not yet dry.
She scrolls a weekly letter to her Nurse
who dares to send a smock through Balthasar,
and once a month, his father posts a purse.
News from Verona? Always news of war.
    Such sour years it takes to right this wrong!
    The fifth act runs unconscionably long.

                                            —Maxine Kumin

4. Study the portrait of Queen Elizabeth from 1600 found on
   the facing page to page 1 in Maurice Hussey's book, *The World
   of Shakespeare and His Contemporaries*, which is aptly subtitled
   A Visual Approach. Note the allegorical eyes and ears. What
   does "fame" report about in your school these days?

5. Study the portrait of Melancholy by Dürer reprinted on page
   29 in Hussey. What is Melancholy thinking? What would
   Hamlet be preoccupied with if he were in your school today?

6. Study the portrait of countryside mummers and of Valentine
   and Orson by Brueghel found on page 40 in Hussey. Describe
   a contemporary sports event which pits antagonists against
   each other, such as boxing, wrestling, or football. Can you
   relate the struggle between good and evil in an event such as
   a wrestling match between Hulk Hogan and Randy Savage
   to Hollywood portrayals of good and evil in Vietnam movies?
   Detective stories? Westerns?

7. Information about fads in clothing, hairstyles, songs, entertainment, and headlines of the day can often be found in
   baby books. Do research in a book such as Grun's *The
   Timetables of History* to construct a baby book for Shakespeare's
   birth year and for your own. Then, spend some time with
   classmates contrasting 1564 with the year of your birth.

** "Purgatory" by Maxine Kumin. From *The Privilege*, by Maxine Kumin (New York:
Harper & Row, 1963) p. 67. Copyright © 1963 by Maxine Kumin.

Students who only see dramas as self-contained works and are reluctant to see them as presentational dramas can address the following questions, perhaps in journal entries, to develop a sense of the dramatic in their own daily lives:

1. Are there times when you remain silent about something, perhaps something about which you feel strongly, in order to avoid a quarrel? In order to avoid giving away your innermost thoughts?

2. Does your inability to express yourself fluently on a particular topic or occasion ever leave you with a feeling of frustration? Does it ever make you say, "Oh, never mind—I can't explain"?

3. Do you ever have to wait so long to speak, or feel so excited emotionally, that you finally say, "I can't remember what I was going to say"?

4. Do certain occasions make you nervous? Do you ever feel as though everything is working out for you? Against you? Does having to give a speech in front of the class make you nervous? Are there certain people who make you feel nervous and others with whom you feel comfortable? Are there some people whose presence is a guarantee to your success or at least feeling of relaxation?

5. Do you ever experience an inner conflict about what you are going to say or do? Does it seem like an inner war?

6. When you are part of an audience, do you ever feel tense or nervous about a developing situation? Does the collective group, the audience, ever function differently than you would if you were observing something alone?

All of these questions and the situations they arise from and lead to can be found in Shakespeare, too. They apply to all of us in our daily lives. Shakespeare allows us to see an image of ourselves on stage. The theatrical image helps us to confront our feelings about these situations.

Aristotle would like the intellectual and moral engagement which can be obtained from the personal, individual experiences of reader response to the text—the fresh, nondoctrinaire responses our young people are capable of. All our students, those who are taking advanced placement history or English, and those who are not so able in school facts but who have intelligence and are looking for a way to express their unspoken enjoyment of literature, would find reader-response criticism a welcoming terrain. After all, some teachers even see their students as living out Shakespearean drama through their conflicts, doubts, feelings of isolation. For these students, literature "becomes a point of contact, an occasion for dialogue" (Walizer 1987, 43). In this case, we return to de Witt's sketch of the Swan, and we realize with the shared pleasure that comes from being part of an interpretive community that we are Shakespeare's audience, too.

———————

Teacher checkpoint. We began with a seemingly simple question: "Who is hiding behind the arras?" We used different answers to that question to review major schools of literary criticism by suggesting ways they would approach and focus on a literary text. The schools include New Criticism, biographical ("intentional") criticism, and approaches which stress literary sources and literary historical context or, more broadly, social and political contexts in which the work was written. We concluded with a look at recent theories such as reader response, feminism, and deconstruction. We also looked at aspects of textual editing; without the work of textual editors, literary critics would have no common, widely available texts to discuss. Finally, we suggested ways that theory can and does enter the classroom.

Notes

1. School systems have always carried on scrutiny of the curriculum but never more intently than in the 1980s in the wake of "A Nation at Risk."

2. Shakespeare's biographer, S. Schoenbaum, calls the dedication a Sphinx which has not met its Oedipus (1977, 269–71).

3. James Hammersmith (1990) sees a shifting away from the Aristotelian model of tragedy, with its emphasis on tragic flaw, toward a more historically rooted view of Elizabethan tragedy with an emphasis on the fall of a great man (*de casibus*) who has a tragic virtue and is entangled in a web of circumstance, and sees it as a critically important paradigmatic shift which as yet is incomplete in public school teaching.

4. *"Ubi sunt"* poems, so called because they often opened with those words, focused on the transitory nature of life.

5. The term, a coinage by Thomas Dekker, referred to the practice by hack authors of refurbishing an old text or text pastiche, not necessarily of their own composition, with new dedications to potential patrons, in hopes of gaining financial reward (Miller 1959, 121).

6. All lines are taken from the Pelican Shakespeare, Alfred Harbage, general editor, except where another edition is specified.

7. It may be necessary to copy more than a line—say, twenty lines. When students recite word-for-word, memorized-by-heart poetry, variations from the text often occur.

8. Speech prefixes are the character names in the margin that indicate which characters speak which lines.

9. *Mimorum aedes* was the designation used by de Witt to mark the wall at the back of the platform stage which furnished the scene, allowed actors to enter and exit, and which also concealed actors' changes of costume.

3 Elizabethan Speech and Shakespearean Language Use

On first looking into classroom Shakespeare, students may look at each other with wild surmise. However, it is unlikely that they feel the awed silence of stout Cortez's men. While the power of nature impresses itself in its grandeur and terror upon our senses immediately, the power of literature may not, especially on the senses of those who were not born New Critics nor have had New Criticism thrust upon them yet. Students whose first acquaintance with Shakespeare is Sonnet 55 ("Not Marble, Nor the Gilded Monuments") may well feel a sense of disappointment, voiceless because of Shakespeare's reputation—which has reached even our fourteen-year-olds in Alabama via Montgomery billboards and teacher sweat shirts, even if by no other means—a reputation dully and dutifully felt. The grounds of the disappointment are hinted at in the polite question, "Is this praise for a woman, or for the poet himself?" When students go further, into the full-immersion baptism of uncut *Romeo and Juliet,* more questions assert themselves, sometimes less politely. Two questions recur: "Did they really talk this way?" and "Why is the plotting so preposterous?" I would like to answer both of these questions for the insistent student questioners who are interested in developing an answer but lack the framework to develop one themselves. In what follows, I will discuss the first question. In chapter 6, I will take up the question of plotting.

The purpose of this chapter is to develop a pedagogical approach to the question, "Did they really talk this way?" The secondary classroom is not the site of experts in the university sense of the word, narrow specialists who research and publish articles on technical points for an audience like themselves. Hence, my purpose is to go beyond a linguistic answer to this question to an awareness in teachers and their students of language and character in drama. Following Charles Barber's practice, when I refer to Elizabethan English, I will mean the "language in Shakespeare's time" (1982, 244); at times, I will refer to evidence from an even slightly earlier time, the 1530s. This, then, would be a more elastic use of the term than the experts would allow. I am also assuming that the student who asks the question about speech is a late twentieth-century American high school student, someone overstimulated by television, videos, movies, and Nintendo, who expects immediate understanding from reading.

For the teacher on the spot, the immediate answer to this student is to focus on the play context in which the question is asked. The teacher of *Romeo and Juliet* has the episodes of that dauntingly long first act blocked out in his or her own mind; it helps to block them out on the blackboard, too. This way lies clarity of answer. If the question originates over Sampson and Gregory's punning, the teacher can answer in a paraphrase of E.A.M. Colman:

> Its sharp contrast with the formality and impressive tone of the prologue sonnet has to be recognized *as* contrast, and it is important that the two idle servingmen are not only joking but are also daring one another into starting a street brawl as soon as opportunity offers. Sex, at this gutter level, is obscurely but intimately mingled with the urge to violence. (1974, 68)

Students are aware of the difference between conversation in the school halls between class periods (analogous to Sampson and Gregory's) and presentations by speakers, perhaps flanked by an array of seated dignitaries on stage at school assemblies in the auditorium (analogous to the Prologue, roughly). If, on the other hand, the students ask about Romeo's behavior as described by his father and by Benvolio, or Romeo's love speeches to Benvolio ("Feather of lead, bright smoke, cold fire, sick health"), the artificiality of his speaking—and the underlying love, really an infatuation—can be stressed. In both of these situations, then, it should be noted that speech varies according to these dimensions:

speaker

situation

audience

speaker's group identification

genre (in this case, subgenres within one drama: Prologue, servant talk, courtly love talk)

Students can become accustomed to such easy terms and develop an intuitive feel for analyzing dramatic material accordingly.

The remainder of this chapter is written for teachers who want more than an on-the-spot answer. I will review one typical classroom strategy for approaching Shakespeare's language; its limitations surface readily. I will then suggest a series of approaches in the classroom, beginning with paper-and-pencil approaches, student acting of scenes, student awareness of variations in character, and finally, linguistic and historical contexts of *Romeo and Juliet.*

We begin this brave enterprise with a few faint-hearted cautions. Clearly, we have no tape recordings of Elizabethan speech as pronounced and spontaneously uttered by sixteenth-century Elizabethans. Also, speech changes over time, even in an age with a strong oral culture. My linguistic and historical examples will be drawn from a long time span, linguistically speaking, from circa 1533 to around 1614. Another difficulty lies in developing a picture of common speech. If by this is meant the speech of ordinary people, we must remind ourselves that the Tudor era, an era of personal, absolutist monarchy, was not democratic. Thus, persistence is required in order to find recorded examples of, say, a yeoman farmer's speech, as is the realization that one might need to turn to offbeat materials such as ecclesiastical court records, for example. Even historicist critics complain that other historicists display an unconscious bias in favor of the monarch and court (Liu 1989, 723), even when purportedly writing about broader points of contact between literature and history. It happens that some written materials exist which will help us develop an intuition of common speech, and those materials will be referred to in the section on linguistic contexts, with proper *caveats* given. Thus, our question about talk becomes, *mutatis mutandi,* a question about writing.

A Typical Classroom Strategy

Some teachers teach Shakespeare—and other literature, too—by focusing on definitions and syllabus/curriculum requirements. This is a formal, not felt, approach to the colors in Shakespeare's coat. So, one way some English teachers have answered any question about Elizabethan speech is to focus on Shakespeare's dramatic poetry, introducing the distinctions among blank verse, rhymed verse, and prose, which in turn necessitates introducing such metrical concepts as iambs and five-foot lines. Often these concepts devolve into such classroom activities as students tapping on desks in time with—or in accidental counterpoint to—the teacher clapping and tapping in front of the class; alternatively, students work on work sheets of excerpted lines, attempting to place soft and accented marks correctly in lines of text, all the while muttering and remuttering lines of blank verse or rhymed verse to themselves. By this point, our muttering tappers have come pretty far from their initial question and may mainly end up frustrated that they have not marked their work sheets correctly. Because of student lack of experience with Shakespearean diction, this may not be a useful way to proceed on first looking into Shakespeare.

Students are capable of feeling these rhythms, and they are capable of the fundamental recognition that poetic verse is not a mimetic copy of speech, but they need a different set of experiences in working with the language first. These experiences are available to them by a combination of means.

Paper Approaches: Structural Grammar, Poetry

The first means is to work through exercises in Shakespeare's word order, omissions, and unusual usages of apparently familiar words provided by Randal Robinson in the NCTE publication *Unlocking Shakespeare's Language* (1988). I like Robinson's approach because his purpose is to sensitize students to Shakespearean language without using numerous grammatical and poetic terms. Robinson's exercises demonstrate a graduated series of points about Shakespeare's language. First, Shakespeare does not always follow the subject-verb-object word order that we in the late twentieth century think of as normal order for clauses in English. Sometimes the verb or object comes first; sometimes an unusual number of modifiers occur before the main clause or between the major sentence elements. The unusual word order may be used to establish patterns of rhyme in a song or speech or to create poetically rhythmical verse. Without relying on technical terms, Robinson (3) says:

> Whenever he was writing blank verse, Shakespeare wrote with a background rhythm in mind, and in writing almost every line, he tried to produce a rhythm that was similar to, although not identical with, the background rhythm. This background rhythm results from a regular alternation of unstressed and stressed syllables. You can create this background rhythm by saying aloud the ten syllables that follow (stress each "DAH" as you read):
>
> da DAH da DAH da DAH da DAH da DAH

Robinson then gives exercises which take the learner through this rhythm in a lived, felt way. As an additional development of Robinson's exercises in syntax, I offer the following series of structural grammatical points taken from Charles Barber's essay on Elizabethan English (1982, 236–43):

1. Elizabethans had choice in adjective formation between *-est* and *most* + simple adjective.

2. Elizabethans had choice between *who/whom* and *which* for persons.

3. Double or multiple negation could be used for emphasis.

4. Elizabethans had regulated choice in the use of "you"/"thou", "thou" being the prerogative of a social superior to use in addressing a social inferior.

5. Elizabethans had choice between *-(e)s,* a colloquial style marker for third-person singular verbs, and *-eth,* part of more solemn and formal speech.

6. Some choice existed in forms of present-tense plural: *-(e)th, -(e)n,* and *-(e)s.*

7. Choice existed for the use of auxiliary *do* in negatives, questions, and emphatic affirmatives.

8. In pronunciation of words, some choice existed for stress patterns, and some vowel combinations had two long vowels. An example of the latter is that "meet" and "meat" were not homonyms. Further, contemporary spelling is a guide—however rough and inexact—to Elizabethan pronunciation.

Students could profitably spend a class period looking for examples of these features in the Shakespearean play they are studying. They might be surprised to learn that books have been written about Elizabethan pronunciation; not only that, several books have been written on Shakespeare's pronoun usage (see point 4. above). The source I consulted, a recent one by Ralph Berry, contains very useful insights on such classroom-relevant topics as Brutus's thoroughly patrician attitude (1988, 146). Even a seemingly small grammatical feature, such as the choice for third-person singular present-tense verb endings, can provide insight into Shakespearean meaning. Consider the following example from Barber:

> In the first scene of *Hamlet,* the forms *has* and *does* occur once each, while *hath* occurs six times and *doth* three. There are seventeen other third-person singular endings in the scene, and all but one are -(e)s—*burns, comes, goes,* etc. The sole exception is the following:
>
>> The bird of dawning *singeth* all night long.
>
> Partly the form *singeth* is chosen for metrical reasons, but it is also to be noticed that it occurs in a particularly solemn and awestruck passage about the mysterious things that occur at Christmas, and this is surely no accident. (1982, 239)

Such is the richness of insight which can be gleaned from grains of grammar.

Listening and Viewing Activities

Two other familiar means to sensitize students to Shakespeare's language are listening to tapes of selected scenes and viewing selected scenes, especially from different versions, in the same class period (Griffin 1989). These activities train student ears and show them that Shakespeare's language can be spoken and understood. Further, it gives them a background rhythm to hear in their own minds. My analogy is modern rap. I know a few talented teachers who have learned to rap, but I know of *none* who have learned to do so without *hearing* spoken examples of rap. (I am waiting to hear of any of my teaching colleagues cutting a rap record.) For students who never quite feel the rhythm of blank verse in listening to it, it may console them to realize that at least one critic asserts that many actors fail to recognize the character of the verse (Sutherland 1970, 76).

Student Acting

The fourth activity in developing student awareness of language and character in drama in general, and in helping students to understand that meaning is expressed and communicated in Shakespearean language, is to have them act out selected scenes. Mike Hayhoe (1989) offers a wealth of suggestions on how to prepare students to do this insightfully. The suggestions include: (1) creative writing as a way of exploring the playwright's alterations from his source in Holinshed for *Macbeth* (Hayhoe supplies a colloquial letter from Holinshed on "knavish errors" of fact to "develop an awareness of how Shakespeare the dramatist turned chronicle into theatre"; (2) a play chart for determining who is on or off stage at a given moment; (3) a game called "And Why?" to help students visualize characters and props; (4) a game called "Put Some Clothes On" to help students visualize and/or design character-appropriate costumes using scraps of clothing; (5) a game called "Make a Scene" which asks students in teams to design two types of stage settings, one for Hollywood and one suited to the students' culture; (6) a game called "Who Goes Where?" which can use graph paper and various-sized three-dimensional markers to show stage placement; (7) a simulation and an activity for casting the play; in the simulation, casting cards are made by students for actors seeking roles in the play; in the casting interview, the students themselves apply for the roles of Duncan, the Porter, etc., and the casting team must justify its choices for the fit between actor and character in the play.

Alfred W. Pollard long ago made the interesting point that the

punctuation of the quarto and folio represents spoken delivery style—
and expresses emotional meaning—better than our modern, logically
and grammatically punctuated texts do ([1917] 1937, xvi–xxii). In spite
of more recent pleas by Charles Frey and others to use old spelling
editions of Shakespeare in the classroom (1984, 554), this has not
occurred. It would be worthwhile on an empirical-testing basis to try
at least isolated passages in speech-pointed punctuation in the classroom.
And, as mentioned earlier, spelling is often, though not infallibly, a
guide to earlier pronunciation. In fact, we may not even be giving the
Bard his accurate name, not if judged by country standards of pronunciation. E.R.C. Brinkworth says that Shakespeare's name was pronounced in Stratford with a short "a" in the first syllable (1972, 34).

A Detour on the Haters of Shakespeare

The activities listed above prepare students to understand and interpret
Shakespeare's plays as dramatic poetry. As poetry, the plays do not
represent spoken language because Elizabethans did not speak rhymed
or blank verse.[1] However, Shakespeare's language has some other
qualities which we can for a moment pretend to filter out from poetic
rhyme and rhythm. These qualities can be recognized by opening the
rather unexpected door of Mark Twain's response to Shakespeare.
Twain, no lover of Shakespeare and in fact enlisted in the rolls of the
anti-Stratfordians, wrote the following parody of speech in Shakespeare:

> Why it ain't *human* talk; nobody that ever lived, ever talked the
> way they do. Even the flunkies can't say the simplest thing the
> way a human being would say it. "Me lord hath given com-
> mandments, sirrah, that the vehicle wherein he doth of ancient
> custom, his daily recreation take, shall unto the portal of the
> palace be straight conveyed; the which commandment, mark ye
> well, admitteth not of wasteful dalliance, like to the tranquil
> mark of yon gilded moon athwart the dappled fields of space,
> but, even as the molten meteor cleaves the skies, or the red-
> tongued bolts of heaven, charged with death, to their dread office
> speed, let this, me lord's commandment, have instant consum-
> mation." (qtd. in L. Levine 1988, 74)

In his essay on *Macbeth,* James Thurber furnishes us with a more
contemporary comment in his persona of the American lady traveler
who looks for a good mystery to read before going to bed and emerges
with this critique:

> "Do you know who discovered Duncan's body?" she demanded.
> I said I was sorry, but I had forgotten. "Macduff discovers it,"

she said, slipping into the historical present. "Then he comes running downstairs and shouts, 'Confusion has broke open the Lord's anointed temple' and 'Sacrilegious murder has made his masterpiece' and on and on like that." The good lady tapped me on the knee. "All that stuff was rehearsed," she said. "You wouldn't say a lot of stuff like that, offhand, would you—if you had found a body?" She fixed me with a glittering eye. "I—" I began. "You're right!" she said. "You wouldn't! Unless you had practiced it in advance. 'My God, there's a body in here!' is what an innocent man would say." She sat back with a confident glare. (1988, 171)

We leave this lady to drink her tea and her interlocutor to his pipe, as we focus on Twain especially. His parody forces us to confront the question of what exactly the intuition of Shakespearean dialogue is in those who are no fans of Shakespeare. The Twain parody demonstrates overelaborateness of speech, a tendency to heavily metaphorize all talk. Twain's reaction is not representative of the majority of our students', but it may represent a tendency of thought in an inexperienced reader. Hence, it is a tendency we are trying to help our students grow beyond. Rather than suppressing any expression of this view, it is healthy to air it, perhaps even to invite it by showing students Twain's parody, and then looking more closely at Shakespeare's own time period—and ours.

Since we have already considered grammatical and metrical qualities of Shakespeare's language, let's return now to the question about speech in *Romeo and Juliet.*

Variations in Character in the Play

When students raise the question about speech very broadly, they can be encouraged to cut their question down to size. Which character are they talking about? In Act I of *Romeo and Juliet,* for example, did Mark Twain, do our students, really think Romeo, Sampson and Gregory, and the Prince speak in exactly the same way? For students who have read several acts, do they think the Romeo of Act II speaks in the same way as the Romeo of Act I? Following are five activities which can help students sensitize themselves to differences in character as reflected in speech.

1. *Students can make a three-column chart* of the speech of different people who are their contemporaries. In the first column, they list some of their contemporaries—a coach, a disc jockey, a newscaster, a teacher, various friends. In column two, students write down something they hear the speaker say. In fact, politicianspeech furnishes ample material, more than is good for our nation. In the third column, students write

a few words characterizing the language of the speaker. Column headings might look like this:

Person   *Statement*   *My description of statement*

Students can then catch the same speaker in an altered mood and write down those words and a description.

2. *School editions sometimes contain excellent suggestions* for introducing students to *Romeo and Juliet*. In the *Elements of Literature, Third Course*, Robert Anderson offers this prereading journal assignment:

> Have students write personal responses to the phrase "love at first sight." What does it mean to them? Do they believe in it? Is *sight* just a metaphor for a complex experience, or is looking somehow more important than other perceptions in romantic love? *Should* it be? (1989, 602)

3. *For their prewriting assignment* accompanying Act II, Anderson asks students to write descriptions of love, using their selection from the following list of words and developing associated images: stars, heaven, eyes, twinkle, daylight, cheek, lamp, vast shore, the farthest sea, wealth, fire, powder, kiss (1989, 629). Additionally, they are asked to specify a speaker and a listener.

4. *Students who are left with the lingering feeling* that Shakespearean characters speak with "one big Elizabethan trumpet" (Sutherland 1970, 76) may even be given quotations before any extended reading assignment and encouraged to discuss what character traits are shown in the statements. Here are some line references and suggested responses:

Romeo I.i.169–80 and I.i.183–93	conventional, artificial
Nurse I.ii.35–48	talkative
Capulet I.v.82–88	genial host, impatient scolder of Tybalt
Juliet I.v.138–41	passionate, committed, emotional, upset

5. *Students may come to better appreciate Romeo's nature* as a conventional courtly lover who actually is somewhat of a figure of fun to Benvolio and Mercutio in Acts I and II if they proceed through the following steps: (1) study a painting such as Nicholas Hilliard's portrait of the lover (Hodges 1980, color plate 7); (2) focus on Benvolio and Lord Montague's early description of Romeo's secretive, moody behavior, Romeo's own artificial love speeches about Rosaline, and Mercutio's jests outside the Capulet garden; (3) study and compare non-Shake-

spearean versions of "young lovers, tragic loss, and cruel destiny" (Cole 1970, 4). That other versions may have elements which are unintentionally funny—and hence, targets for parody—will be immediately understood by students when they are told that Shakespeare's source for *Romeo and Juliet*, Arthur Brooke's *The Tragical History of Romeo and Juliet*, includes a falling-in-love scene in which three people are present, Mercutio on one side, Romeo on the other, Juliet in the middle, her hand held first by the one, then by the other (112). Our students can very well sense the absurdity of this scene. A caution, however: they should not conclude that Shakespeare is parodying Romeo and Juliet's love, but rather that pale shadow love of Romeo for Rosaline!

Since all literary forms operate with conventions, it would be worthwhile to help students develop an instinctive sense of this term. They can be brought to an awareness of the meaning of the word "convention" by discussing the verbal conventions of such familiar forms as rock videos, sportscasting and sports interviews, wrestling threats and counterthreats, and rapping. All have conventions, and all are subject to imitation, clever or not so clever, parodic or good humored. Anyone who doubts this should view Weird Al Yankovich's videos parodying Michael Jackson, or roller derby's sportscasters' parody of more conventional sportscasting, or McDonald's commercials which imitate black rappers.

Common Language Background of *Romeo and Juliet*

Some sources exist for helping us develop our intuition of the speech of Shakespeare's fellow Elizabethans in the absence of either Elizabethan tape recorders or perfected, modern day, time-traveling machines. Such sources include court testimony, contemporary letters, jestbooks and jokebooks, personal commonplace books, information about London "lowlife," and scholarly research on the topics of both bawdy and proverbs.

Maurice Evans researched parliamentary debates and court cases at a variety of levels to find verbatim reports of authentic speech, deliberately eschewing turning to drama itself. Because I agree with this approach, I would like to note his conclusions about the speech he surveyed. In regard to uneducated speech as revealed in village ecclesiastical trials, he noted its "unusually explosive quality" joined with "a fine command of picturesque words and phrases" as well as "dramatic qualities" and "variation in tone" but also its formlessness in long stretches. In educated speakers, he notes, "The vigorous colloquial power is still apparent, and there are plenty of illustrations, of pithy similitudes or bold and earthy jests which have their origin in the speech of common men." He also found "educated Elizabethan English . . . remarkable for its flexibility and clarity . . . simplicity and directness" (1951, 403–06). In addition to noting a range of moods and tempos, and the presence of controlled irony (preeminently in a speaker such as Walter Raleigh), he enumerated the following characteristics:

1. "the influence of the Bible"
2. the use of Latin or Latin tags
3. puns, even from dignified speakers on serious occasions
4. variations on a stock of common metaphors but *not* "heavily metaphorical like dramatic language"
5. use of short, well-known images
6. proverbs
7. only a rare recourse to "witty speech"

In fact, he concluded that common speech with its unrhetorical character eventually contributed to the formation of scientific expression which seventeenth-century prose worked towards (410–13).

Testimony in ecclesiastical courts, even that in Stratford itself, shows that the explosive language of, say, Mercutio, the Prince's kinsman, was not confined to the stage. He was not the only one to invoke plagues on people. Appearing before the Stratford court on October 1, 1595, one Elizabeth Wheeler exclaimed, "God's wounds, a plague of God on you all, a fart on one's arse for you" (qtd. in Brinkworth 1972, 63). One wonders how this character would have fared in an acquaintance with a real-life Mercutio. This gives sense to Romeo's "O brawling love."

John Chamberlain, Shakespeare's contemporary and a letter writer, records this instance of speech in a letter dated December 9, 1608, to his friend Dudley Carleton, on whose behalf Chamberlain was interceding:

> I went to the idle oracle of the Strand on Saturday to see what was become of your letter, . . . who told me it was not yet delivered. . . . Whereupon seeing me discontented he brake out into this protestation, "God is my judge, I am as careful of it as yourself," and so we parted. (Thomson, 1965, 64–65)

One wonders if the next words from Sir Walter Cope, excused by his own wife for "age, want of memory, and multiplicity of business," would resemble the Nurse's to Juliet: "Henceforward do your messages yourself" (65).

The Lisle letters, a collection from earlier in the Tudor period, dating from 1533 to 1540, contain two interesting representations of speech which can be applied to *Romeo and Juliet*. The Nurse's garrulousness has long been recognized as part of her character. What may be surprising to the anti-Stratfordians who argue that Shakespeare, a commoner, could not have known the speech of kings and nobles, is the representation of the king's counselor's intimate speech found in Lisle #111, dated October 17, 1534:

> With that answered Mr. Secretary in this manner, "The King's Grace being his good lord, say you? Yes, marry, I warrant you, he is and will be his good lord. His good lord, quod a! Marry, he may be sure he is and will be his good lord. Doubt ye not of that." And thus he repeated it, iij or iiij times, that the King's Highness was and would be good lord unto your lordship. (Byrne 1981, 137)

So, Thomas Cromwell repeated himself, too, not very unlike our Nurse.

Friar Laurence's exclamation "Benedicite!" and other speeches have led some critics to see him as an apt portrait of a cleric. What shall we say when we see this line in one of servant John Husee's letters (Lisle #213, dated May 18, 1538) to Lady Lisle, his employer:

> Howbeit, to be plain with your ladyship, I think that money would make her wife to Sir Edward Baynton's son and heir. But this is under Benedicite. (245)

The Queen's jester Dick Tarlton's jestbook contains the following story:

> How *Tarlton* and one in the Gallery fell out. It chanced that in the midst of a Play, after long expectation for *Tarlton*, being much desired of the people, at length hee came forth. Where (at his entrance) one in the Gallerie pointed his finger at him, saying to a friend that he had never seene him, That is he. *Tarlton*, to make sport at the least occasion given him, and seeing the man point with one finger, he in love againe held up two fingers: the captious fellow, jealous of his wife (for he was married) and because a Player did it, took the matter more hainously, and asked him why he made hornes at him? No (quoth *Tarlton*) they be fingers:
>
>> For there is no man, which in love to me,
>> Lends me one finger, but he shall have three,
>
> No, no sayes the fellow, you gave me the hornes. True (sayes *Tarlton*) for my fingers are tipt with nailes, which are like hornes, and I must make a shew of that which you are sure of. This matter grew so, that the more he medled the more it was for his disgrace; wherefore the standers by counselled him to depart, both hee and his hornes, lest his cause grow desperate. So the

poore felow, plucking his hat over his eyes, went his wayes. (qtd.
in Gurr 1987, 126)

Tarlton performed in the 1580s. This scene of Tarlton outwitting a man
in the gallery is quoted for the indirect light it sheds on Sampson's
thumb biting at Abram; hand gestures and verbal insults went together.

Commonplace books, collections of miscellaneous materials which
interested their authors, were like our modern-day diaries. Thomas
Fella's commonplace book, the product of this Suffolk merchant's spare-
time sketching and writing over the period 1585–1622, provides valuable
insights into country life. Peasant dialogue as shown in the sketchbook
is extremely simple. Consider, for example, the month of December
(reproduced in Schoenbaum 1979, 38). A rustic is cooking swine by
the victualing house; elsewhere, people are baking bread. One says: "I
cannot gitt the dirte p-paft of my hands." The workers in Shakespeare's
Capulet kitchen speak with more saucy cunning than these rustics.

The diary of law student John Manningham calls our attention
to the poem "it is merry when Gossips meete" (Sorlien 1976, 98). When
Capulet angrily directs the Nurse "Smatter with our gossips, go!" he is
contemptuously dismissing her to the fun of idle talk and the "gossip's
bowl." The following little dialogue recorded by Manningham might
remind us of Juliet's outburst against Romeo ("O serpent heart, hid
with a flow'ring face!"), uttered when the Nurse misinforms her about
Tybalt's death:

> One said of a foule face, "it needs noe maske, it is a maske it
> selfe." "Nay," said an other, "it hath neede of a maske to hide
> the deformitie." (121)

As a law student, Manningham was training his ear for dialogue, and
this trait shows throughout his diary.

Robert Greene, that splenetic consumer of deathly quantities of
pickled herrings and Rhenish wine (Schoenbaum 1977, 149), has
furnished us with much of the argot of London's thieves, as well as
with a hint about country pronunciation—a voice that is "nothing
gracious" (qtd. in Nicoll 1957, 65). In his "A pleasant discovery of the
cozenage of colliers," Greene furnishes several instances of the cunning
thievery of coal carriers, ending with the story of one forced to submit
to a mock court of sixteen women, "tried by the verdict of the smock"
and forced to submit to a beating in spite of his bold-faced "God speed
you all, shrews!" and attempt to leave (qtd. in Judges 1930, 143–49).
What is most remarkable about Greene's presentation versus Shakespeare's is the latter's notable compression of language, being quick

and allusive rather than labored and lengthily explanatory. This, perhaps, increases Shakespeare's difficulty for the novice reader.

The topic of Shakespeare's bawdy requires tact on the part of the secondary teacher. Unbowdlerized texts are now available for the first time in classroom anthologies, though they sometimes lack explanatory footnotes to archaic bawdy (not all of which has acquired the patina of a venerable antique; some of it is dusted off daily in the mouths of some speakers). My main comment about the thematic purpose of bawdy in *Romeo and Juliet* is that the coarse, racy comments of such characters as Mercutio, the Nurse, and even Juliet's own father serve as a contrast to make the love of Romeo and Juliet for each other seem finer, better, and more complete than the earthy physicality that these other speakers connect with love. This in no way denies the physical component of the young lovers' feelings for each other. Teachers who are unsure about individual elements of bawdy may consult the list of words with a double entendre in William Betken's edition of *Romeo and Juliet* (1984, 459–62), or they may refer to Eric Partridge's book, *Shakespeare's Bawdy.*

Of our school tragedies, Partridge classifies *Julius Caesar* as the "cleanest historical play" next to *Richard II* and *Macbeth* as marked by "comparative innocuousness" and *Hamlet* and *Romeo and Juliet* as bawdy, relatively speaking. A more useful approach can be found in E.A.M. Colman, who asks of scenes or parts within scenes, "Why is this here?" The usefulness of this approach can be seen in his comment on the Nurse's speech upon discovering Juliet in Act IV after Juliet has taken the potion furnished by Friar Laurence:

> Even though the theatre audience knows well enough that Juliet is not really dead, there is suspense in awaiting discovery of the *supposed* death, and this is heightened by the protracted sense of the ordinary, the humdrum, that the Nurse's prurience maintains. It is a Chekhovian effect. . . . The Nurse's speech as she tries to waken Juliet forms a small but typical part of the world of accident, muddle and human mediocrity to which the lovers fall victim. (1974, 72)

I don't think all the bawdy meanings need to be spelled out for secondary students, nor do our school anthology writers. However, students will sense some meanings on their own. The point is, they know bawdy exists in real life, in the halls, on school buses, in graffiti, in comments the teacher does not hear. The wise teacher will become informed about local school district censorship policy, as well as NCTE policy statements and guidelines on censorship challenges to school curricula.

The final item in our language survey centers on the proverb. Proverbs prove elusive of definition, although I like James Howell's definition that "the chief Ingredients that go to make a true Proverb are *Sense, shortnesse* and *Salt*" (qtd. in Dent 1981, xii). To understand their significance as character markers, students need to think of some of our idiomatic expressions: putting something on the back burner, out of the frying pan and into the fire, the pot calling the kettle black, calling a spade a spade, etc. Students may have difficulty with this task because our textbooks in grammar and composition labor so arduously to stamp out cliché, lack of originality, anything that smacks of the pathways of folk thought. Such is our legacy from the Romantics. By R. W. Dent's tally, proverbs prove to be especially significant for *Romeo and Juliet*, for the play has the most proverbial language of any of Shakespeare's works. Moreover, its use of proverbs exceeds that of *Julius Caesar's* by a ratio of over three to one and of *Macbeth's* by over two to one. A good close-reading activity for students is to have them try to identify proverbial-sounding language from the text and then verify it by Dent's index (1981, 24–34; see also Dent's appendixes, 45–284 for the expressions themselves). An example of something which sounds proverbial is Mercutio's "They have made worms' meat of me," and in fact it is, in variant form, "A man is nothing but worms' meat," dating back to circa 1400 (166). Part of the fun in exploring proverbs in Shakespeare comes in identifying them and after that, in seeing whether they are retained today, and why or why not. A human now is more likely to be referred to as a collection of chemicals worth around $1.98 (I haven't allowed for inflation from when I first heard this some years back), which reflects our greater scientific awareness—and focus on the material and physical now, rather than on *memento mori* images. One proverbial image which has survived as a book title is Sampson's reference to women as the "weaker vessels." This image, which had currency in Elizabethan England and which has a Biblical analogue in 1 Peter 3:7, is found in Antonia Fraser's book about women in the seventeenth century, *The Weaker Vessel.* The final task students can attempt is to see whether certain characters are more likely than others to rely on proverbs in formulating their thoughts.

Historical Contexts of *Romeo and Juliet*

Rhetorical/Metaphorical Age

The Elizabethan era respected the rhetorical and the metaphorical. That era occurred before the heavy emphasis on plain style—both oral and written, advocated by Puritans and scientists in the seventeenth century—gained ascendancy. T. S. Eliot's famous formulation of this shift is that a "dissociation of sensibility" occurred some time after the English Renaissance and before the completion of the Industrial Revolution, a dissociation making it all but impossible for many twentieth-century readers to read early modern poetry with an appreciation for the sensibility that informs it. In a somewhat different formulation, Walter Ong sees the radical change in sensibility as consisting in a shift from the oratorical to the neutral (1971, 65). A slightly different aspect of this oral/rhetorical character is seen in Muriel St. Clare Byrne's assertion that even small events in ordinary life in the Elizabethan period did not go unmarked by the alert observers of that time:

> Free of the de-vitalizing high-pressure attack forced today upon the ordinary man's natural sensitivity by mass-media of entertainment, instruction, and solicitation, the Elizabethan eye and ear had an alertness of response that we now dull or dissipate by over-stimulation. To jog another's forgetfulness men would recreate the living detail of setting and circumstances to recall exactly what had happened or had been said, because they had really seen and heard. (1966, 202)

This point is reinforced by Ong's reading of Elizabeth Eisenstein's book on the enormous significance of the printing press in modern life, especially in the construction of notions of the self. Ong notes a greater interiority and isolation of the individual as a result of the printing press and attendant literacy (1982, 130–32).

Pedagogy

The teacher can explore these issues with students. First, find passages in Shakespeare where an event is described, not enacted on stage, but which nonetheless seems like a scene to the readers. An example is Casca's report of Caesar's speech to the rabble and Caesar's epileptic fit. Other examples are the Nurse's report of Juliet's "sententious" statements about Romeo and rosemary, Macbeth's report of the image of Duncan's dead body and his slaying of the guilty grooms, and Gertrude's report of Ophelia's drowning. Second, students can find passages in Shakespeare where one character urges another to give voice to inner feelings. An example is Malcolm's urging of Macduff to do so on receiving news of the deaths of his wife and children. Third, invite students to reflect on the ways printed matter both divides and unites us. Without print, how would the experience of learning to read and to write be different? (If "r" is for "rosemary," then "h" surely is for "hornbook.") Here is a series of questions to direct to students:

1. What feelings do you have in periods of silent reading?

2. Do you like to get "lost" in a book? Or are you one of those people who say, "I hate to read"? If so, is it because you prefer sports, music, the beach, or some other activity?

3. Do you ever feel like disturbing the silence in class during silent reading?

4. How do you view times when the class goes to the library? As an opportunity to move around? As an opportunity to socialize and sit with friends? As an opportunity to outwit teacher and librarian? As an opportunity to find interesting reading?

5. On your view of drama as a specific printed form, would you understand Shakespeare better by listening to the class read sections without following in your book? With following? By silent reading?

6. Do you like plays as a form of reading? If so, is it because they seem lifelike? Is it because plays allow speech, movement, and involvement by more than one person?

Metaphor can be found in letters; memorable remarks by such popular public figures as Shakespeare's clown, Will Kempe, or the Queen's jester, Richard Tarlton; quips by the Queen on ceremonial public occasions as well as more intrinsically urgent occasions such as her address to the troops at Tilbury; sermons; jokes in prose; speeches to parliament; and trial testimony. Although Maurice Evans does not find extended metaphors or elaborate wit play in his examination of parliamentary speeches or court testimony, I think we would find even less recourse to metaphor in ordinary speech or in public performances today. Sometimes, as in the case of President Bush's figure of the "thousand points of light" during his presidential campaigning, the metaphor becomes a figure of fun for reporters and public alike.

Age of Listening

The Elizabethan public had ears trained for oral performances, not just functional utterances. Andrew Gurr makes the point that the earliest word used for Shakespeare's and other playwrights' public theatre audiences was the word "auditors," a word which emphasizes the oral character of the plays and their reception. After around 1600, the word which is used increasingly for the audience is "spectators," a word which emphasizes the visual quality of the theatre, most notably of the masques, which drew from Ben Jonson the grousing judgment that they were "painting and carpentry plays" (Gurr 1987, 85–86).

Audience practice of the virtue of patience was reinforced by various auditory experiences. Sermon listeners at St. Paul's Cross sometimes heard a sermon three hours long, with perhaps 5,000 in the audience (Hussey 1978, 32). The Sunday Elizabethan church service, even in Stratford, was two hours long (Brinkworth 1972, 15). Foreign visitors observed people in church in the early seventeenth century taking notes on the sermon for later discussion at home. The diarist and law student John Manningham has notes, on occasion running to thirteen pages, on many sermons. Grammar school education had a heavy oral component; each day the class would listen to a passage in Latin pronounced by the schoolmaster. Conjugations were practiced and tested orally. Universities conducted final examinations orally. The final test of the candidate about to become a Bachelor was

> certain climactic disputations called "Determinations." This was the arduous part of becoming a Bachelor, for he had to stand against all comers who chose to oppose him on logical or philosophical questions; and this he had to do during most of the days of Lent. (Thompson, 1962, 348).

All of these experiences encouraged good habits of listening. One wonders, what was young Hamlet writing in his memory book? By way of contrast with today's students, we can note that we have many good students who do not score particularly well on the listening portion of standardized, school-administered tests. We live in an age of saturated ears as well as saturated fats.

Listening, however, may be an incomplete means for absorbing a Shakespearean drama, so we now turn to how and why Shakespeare's plays were at first published in stolen form. People from Shakespeare's own time who saw his plays and made notes on them usually confined their comments to matters of plot. At least one book purchaser made the comment that he bought a quarto so as to be better able to look over the words of a play at his leisure. Even in Elizabethan times, one hearing of *Hamlet* may not have been sufficient to take it all in.

Earlier theories of the means of transmission of Shakespeare's pirated texts focus on the possibility of a shorthand transcription having been made during a performance. Timothy Bright published a book on *Characterie* (subtitled *An Arte of Shorte, swifte, and secrete writing by character*) in 1588. However, the level of shorthand knowledge represented by Bright would have been inadequate to have resulted in a complete text stenographically reported.

An improved system of shorthand was introduced by John Willis in his *Stenography* in 1602, but the pirated *Romeo and Juliet* was printed in 1597, with the good quarto appearing in 1599. As a personal note, I can testify, as someone who earned the Gregg 140 words per minute (wpm) pin in high school, to the near impossibility of transcribing a Shakespeare text in this manner. If average speech is uttered at the rate of 180 wpm, many words would be lost each minute.[2]

A somewhat better theory of the origin of the pirated texts is the "memorial reconstruction" theory, which holds that an actor or actors dictated the play to a printer from memory. The best recent theories focus on some form of text being given the printer, i.e., the author's foul papers, a transcription from them, or the playhouse prompt book. (Stanley Wells says the Folio *Julius Caesar* and *Macbeth* are from prompt copy copied by King's Men's scrivener Ralph Crane and the *Romeo and Juliet* good quarto is from foul papers [1984, 59, 74].)

Pedagogy

The teacher can try student transcription from tapes in whatever form students care to write their transcriptions as an activity. This promises to be fun, raucous, and short in endurance. Also, students can discuss current entertainment technologies and copyright laws, such as records and pirated tapes, movies and VCR copies, and copyright of ideas. Such a discussion will help students to understand the bootlegger's impulse—and the audience appetite it feeds upon. Further, invite students to reflect on Michael Jackson or Stevie Wonder in the recording studio, or actor-playwright Michael Douglas on the Hollywood set. How likely is it that such busy, entertainment-production oriented individuals would sit quietly over final copies of manuscripts destined for printers, carefully tidying up spelling, punctuation, and other English teacher concerns. Because "mistakes" in such scenes as *Julius Caesar* IV.iii., which seems to involve more than one reporting of Portia's death, have suggested to critics the possibility of Shakespeare revising but not having the revisions accurately carried forward by scribe or printer, students may also take delight in reflecting on their own composition habits and revision processes. Do they ever have a parent, boyfriend, or girlfriend type a paper for them and do so incorrectly or make changes in their text? To understand why bad quartos of such plays as *Romeo and Juliet* and *Hamlet* were followed by good, corrected quartos, students might be interested in studying a contemporary copyright law case, such as Art Buchwald's suit against Eddie Murphy, to understand Shakespeare's feeling about pirated texts and the form in which he took action. Students might also note that popular movies such as the *Star Wars* trilogy or *Karate Kid* series not only spawn other movies but also books which tell the story (novelizations). Phrases such as "Use the Force!" enter into popular consciousness.

Finally, students can reflect on and/or write a journal entry about their own listening habits: Do they listen to parents, teachers, preachers, speeches by public figures, news reports, attentively? Do they listen to music and song lyrics attentively? Critically?

Age of the Dramatic

The Elizabethan era had a sense of the dramatic. Recent historians emphasize the leading role taken by the Queen herself in her ornate clothing, the studied "naturalness" and brilliance of her speeches, the elaborately ceremonial nature of her court, her public progresses. Clothing, in an age which had Sumptuary Laws restricting the wearing of certain colors, fabrics, and furs according to social status, was so important that it was worth faking being in the household of a great person:

> The livery of a great lord had a cash value. . . . In 1593 Charles Chester offered the Earl of Essex's steward Gelli Meyrick £100 "if you will procure me my lord's cloth." (Stone 1967, 102)

Hence, talk in *Romeo and Juliet* of Juliet casting off the "vestal livery" of the moon, or, more to the point, Mercutio's angry denial to Tybalt that Romeo wears his livery, is not mere poetic dreaminess, but relevant to Elizabethan social concerns. Shakespeare himself and his company were issued three or four yards of bastard scarlet[3] to wear as liveried King's Men in a procession honoring James I on his accession to the English throne.

One retained one's sense of the dramatic even unto death. Stephen Greenblatt, biographer of the dashing Sir Walter Raleigh, stresses the artful in Raleigh's execution: his use of nonfatal ointments and vomit-inducing agents which produced a disease-like state in him, not far from King Hamlet's lazar-like crust, in an attempt to postpone his beheading in 1618; his careful emending of a poem written years earlier; his delivery of a death speech which lasted three-quarters of an hour (1973, 4, 12–14, 20).

Many prominent people were executed during the Tudor and Stuart reigns. It is interesting to note their final words. Perhaps these words will help students to recognize the strong impulse to oral performance (not intended here in the sense of something false) in the

Elizabethan time period, and thus not to be so disparaging or jesting about characters' protracted death speeches. (In fact, students like Mercutio so well that they don't begrudge him the seventeen-plus lines it takes for his dispatch.)

John Fisher, Bishop of Rochester, for example, made this statement in seeking some comfort from his Bible as he awaited sheriffs who would take him to his beheading:

> Oh Lord, this is the last time that I shall ever open this book, let some comfortable place now chance to me, whereby I, Thy poor servant, may glorify Thee in this my last hour. (qtd. in Hibbert 1971, 51)

Fisher's use of the word *comfortable* antedates and resembles Juliet's sense of the word in her remark to Friar Laurence upon awakening in the Capulet tomb: "O comfortable friar! where is my lord!" (V.iii.148). Fisher's statement to his executioner contains a simple metaphor in the use of the word *storm:* "I forgive thee with all my heart, and I trust thou shalt see me overcome this storm with courage" (qtd. in Hibbert 1971, 51).

The use of gentle humor is seen in Thomas More's steady courage, dignity, and wit at his execution. He addressed these remarks to one of the guards: "I pray thee see me safely up, but as for my coming down again, let me shift for myself." To the executioner, he said: "Let me lay my beard over the block lest you cut it, for *it* has never committed treason" (qtd. in Hibbert 1971, 52). These lines help us understand Romeo's lines on entering the Capulet tomb with the body of Paris:

> How oft when men are at the point of death
> Have they been merry! which their keepers call
> A lightning before death.
>
>   (V.iii.88–90)

The same "lightning" is seen in Hugh Latimer, Bishop of Worcester, when fortune in her turnings brought him to the drafty Tower to await a death by burning at the stake. He observed to the guards: "I suppose you expect me to be burned, but unless you let me have some fire, I am likely to deceive your expectations, for I shall most probably die of the cold" (qtd. in Hibbert 1971, 76).

Juliet's seeming welcoming of death might be seen in the acceptance of the inevitable shown by Anne Boleyn. The Constable of the Tower, Sir William Kingston, reported:

> I have seen many men, and also women executed, and they have been in great sorrow, but, to my knowledge, this lady has much

joy and pleasure in death. Her almoner is continually with her, and has been today since two of the clock after midnight. (qtd. in Hibbert 1971, 59)

Finally, the words of Lady Frances Howard, Countess of Somerset, upon her arrest for the murder of Sir Thomas Overbury and her jailor's attempt to incarcerate her in the cell in the Tower where she had systematically poisoned Sir Thomas, are instructive: "Put me not in there; his ghost will haunt me!" (qtd. in Hibbert 1971, 92). Though Frances's character is very unlike Juliet's, these words of hers remind us of Juliet's fears before taking Friar Laurence's potion:

> O look! methinks I see my cousin's ghost
> Seeking out Romeo, that did spit his body
> Upon a rapier's point. Stay, Tybalt, stay!
>
> (IV.iii.55–57)

Lady Frances's words were accompanied by shrieking (from her) and near fainting (by her). Juliet's innocence stands in radical contrast to the ruthless Frances, whose systematic assault on the unsuspecting Overbury makes for bloodcurdling reading. The reader can be introduced to Frances Howard's character by the following inventory of pharmaceuticals:

> To his cell in the Bloody Tower she sent poisoned tarts and poisoned jellies; she had his wine poisoned with mercury sublimate, his partridges with lapis costitus; she had white and red arsenic mixed with his salt, cantharides with his pepper, and lunar caustic (silver nitrate) with his pork. She plied him with "Great Spiders" and aqua fortis (nitric acid) and powdered diamonds. (Hibbert 1971, 92)

The curious reader can learn in detail about Lady Howard's motives and machinations in Beatrice White's *Cast of Ravens*. Howard clearly was a Paracelsian, a believer in the use of metals, rather than a Galenist, a believer in humors and bloodletting, in her medical propensities.

Lest the reader be left with the impression that the Elizabethan sense of the dramatic was unrelievedly doleful and lugubrious, I close this account of the age of the dramatic with two anecdotes which show two forms of Elizabethan wit—the robust and the delicate. Thomas Lodge's often-quoted comment about a precursor to Hamlet makes us wonder about the sounds resonating from the theatre to passersby, when he referred to the ghost crying out on stage "like an oister wife, 'Hamlet revenge!'" (qtd. in Campbell and Quinn 1966, 462). The other remark which historians are especially fond of quoting comes to us from Bishop Godfrey Goodman, reporting on the love and admiration felt by a crowd which had been waiting for the Queen on seeing her finally emerge from council chambers at night. Although Goodman acknowledges that they would have hazarded their lives for the Queen at that moment, he also wryly observes that "show and pageants are ever best seen by torchlight" (qtd. in Smith 1975, 80).

Pedagogy

Students can reflect on how clothing—whether it is sloppy, casual, or stylish—is not only part of their self-image but also part of their self-presentation to others.

Charney notes:

> The Elizabethans were much more given to symbolism that we are, not only in literature, but also in their daily life. Clothes, for example, indicated a man's occupation and social position in a very specific, traditional way. We should also consider the emblematic nature of such daily items as colors, jewels, embroidery, heraldic badges and mottoes, and the posies of rings. (1961, 198)

Students can assemble pictures from magazines of how some contemporary people's clothing still indicates occupation and/or social position (e.g., priest, minister, rabbi, nun, nurse, doctor, veterinarian, worker in overalls, fast food worker, stockbroker and banker, person in armed services, police officer, person "dressing for success"). Further, they can study portraits of the Queen—like the coronation portrait (Fox 1972, 70) or the Armada portrait (Smith 1967, 275)—and write analyses of the messages conveyed by these portraits.

Also, students can draw on the intimacy of sitting for a Renaissance portrait and write a vignette about the sitting, one in which they bring out character details about the painter (such as Holbein) or the limnist (such as Nicholas Hilliard), descriptive details of the portrait, and character details of the subject of the portrait.

Age of Censorship

Graham Greene has described the surface of Shakespeare's plays as "smooth and ambiguous" (1951, xi). Shakespeare has often been described as our most impersonal writer; drama itself is an impersonal medium. These features, which can be perceived as a puzzling objectivity on the part of the dramatist, may be accounted for in part by the censorship of Shakespeare's time.

To begin with Henry VIII, the Lisle letters (a collection of letters written by and to Arthur Plantagenet, Lord Lisle, an illegitimate son of

Edward IV, and his family members from 1533 to 1540—which have survived as a valuable historical source because of their seizure as evidence against Lord Lisle by Henry's agents in Calais in 1540) contain explicit pleas by Lisle's agent, John Husee, to exercise prudent restraint in writing, as in #23, dated September 20, 1534:

> Also Mr. Bryan willed me to write further to your lordship that you must keep things secreter than you have used, and saith that there is nothing done nor spoken but it is with speed knowen in the Court. (Byrne 1981, 45)

Husee also expressed a desire to be excused from the obligation of expressing news in writing:

> there is divers here that hath been punished for reading and copying with publishing abroad of news; yea, some of them are at this hour in the Tower and like to suffer therefore.... It is much better that I stay from writing than to put your lordship to displeasure and myself to undoing. (154)

The letters also contain the frequent statement that other news is carried by the bearer of the letter. Even those outside the main channels of intrigue fear invasions of their private letters or miscarried letters. Jane Basset, for example, from a place in the English countryside, writes thus to her mother in #230, dated March 12, 1536: "Write ye unto them by parables, as though he knew nothing of this, because of the saving of my writer harmless of displeasure" (259).

In this atmosphere of spying and suspicion, it is perhaps not surprising that in 1534 an Act for the Succession "made it high treason maliciously to deny or attack the Anne Boleyn marriage" (Byrne 1981, 74), nor is it surprising that even in 1547 when the King was visibly declining it was "high treason to prophesy the King's death" (Hibbert 1971, 65).

Queen Elizabeth also imposed restrictions on speech. For example, in 1579 two of her court ladies were arrested for discussing the possibility of her marriage to the Duke of Alençon (J. Levine 1969, 108). The Master of Revels—a position which dates back in weakened form to 1494 but which became a more formidable position of government exercise of control during the term of Edmund Tilney, from 1579 to 1609—passed judgment on the suitability of plays to be performed before court and general audiences as well. In 1599, books by such authors as Thomas Nashe and Gabriel Harvey, books which could be characterized as satires and ribald works, were burned "in Elizabeth's greatest bonfire of books" (Miller 1959, 191) for deviation in matters of religious doctrine and for challenges to the government.

Challenges to the government continued to be punishable offenses during James's reign. The outcome of the sensational Overbury murder trial mentioned earlier was that the lesser figures implicated in the plot—the suppliers and purveyors of the poison—were executed, while Frances Howard received a royal pardon! Merely to ask one Richard Weston, as he was traveling in a cart to Tyburn for hanging, whether he was guilty as charged was in itself an arrestable offense, "traducing the public justice," for it constituted a threat to the orderly carrying out of the law, and several who did were "arraigned . . . in *camera stellata*"[4] (White 1967, 117–18).

In the year 1631, the printer of the so-called "wicked Bible," which omitted the "not" from the seventh commandment, was fined for his error (Eisenstein 1979, 81).

In addition, the reach of the ecclesiastical courts into the individual's private life is unknown and unknowable today. Individuals in Stratford, for example, were brought to the local church court, presided over by the vicar, for a range of offenses which included swearing; slander; nonattendance at church services or catechism lessons; playing cards, drinking, dancing, or working during service time or on a holy day; sexual misconduct; and sorcery. Depending on the severity of the offense, punishment could be public and humiliating:

> The aim of the Judge in ordering penance was to make the punishment fit the crime. A fully public penance was conducted by the minister standing in the pulpit. The penitent was required to confess the sin in intimate detail, standing on a stool in the middle aisle near the pulpit, clad either in ordinary clothes or, for the most serious offences, enveloped in a white sheet, bareheaded, barefooted, and holding a white rod. The length of time varied too: some had to stand for the whole length of the service, some until the end of the sermon, some only until the end of the second lesson. Some had to do penance on more than one Sunday; some in the Gild Chapel as well as the church. Some in addition had to suffer the shame of a white sheet penance in the Market Place. Thursday is often mentioned. It was then the weekly Market Day. (Brinkworth 1972, 15)

Pedagogy

Students can be encouraged to consider this material in the following ways:

1. They should explore what difference this atmosphere of control made to Shakespeare's plays. For example, in considering the Prince's task at the end of *Romeo and Juliet*—i.e., to decide

who shall be pardoned and who punished—my students have found that their view of the guilt or innocence of various parties in the play shifts depending on what director's version of the play's events we have seen. Perhaps Shakespeare's indirection was in part a result of the censor's hand and eye. Was the Prince "winking at . . . discords" a figure of Elizabeth? Students enjoy mock trials. They can script a court inquiry into the various parties' responsibilities. Now, whether it is a Star Chamber inquiry or a more open courtroom will make all the difference to the outcome. Even this issue can be explored.

2. Students can contrast our own free speech atmosphere and related free speech issues, both to understand their own period and to understand the Elizabethan period better. Have we gained in quality by removing restraints from the presentation of sexual issues? Free speech issues related to education and to minors are fascinating; I have generally found these issues to be of interest to all ability levels in the classroom. I have used both the legal pages of *The Kappan* and current news reports of legal issues in newspapers and *Newsweek*. In addition, the *English Journal* has on occasion had material related to free speech issues in its articles.

3. As a related matter, documented cases of swearing or personal unkindness to another plus a required public penance/apology are occurrences in classrooms. Students can explore their feelings. Hamlet complained that Denmark was a prison. Sometimes itching high school seniors complain that school is a prison. Restive students might want to address this issue. Students who are not of so choleric or melancholy a humor might enjoy creating an imaginary assistant principal's file of office referrals.

Conclusion

The Bodleian First Folio, chained in the early seventeenth century in the Oxford Library's reading room because of the costliness of books then, shows a well-thumbed *Romeo and Juliet* balcony scene, much like our library globes here present a well-rubbed state of Alabama. These young Oxford undergraduates, these boys away from home, training for a social position, what did they see in that scene?

I think they saw the same thing we do: a lyrically expressed love, beautiful and fine, almost cosmic and outside of time, emerging from the easy, casual vulgarity of the rest of society. Seeing this love took them, at least for the moment, out of the restrictions imposed on them by society—the life of convention, expectation, duties, responsibilities, obligations.

We can help our students see the same qualities in this scene. But of course, they do even without our help. When my students memorize lines from *Romeo and Juliet,* they almost invariably turn to this scene. A few bossy souls memorize the Prince's scolding order to the Veronese; a few very shy ones memorize Romeo's II.ii soliloquy, his heart in hiding; some madcaps memorize Mercutio; a few real actors memorize Sampson and Gregory complete with thumb-biting gestures— but the majority talk the love talk of Romeo and Juliet at the balcony.

———

Teacher checkpoint. We began with a student-posed question about the dialogue in Shakespearean drama, often raised in a spirit of exasperation: "Did they really talk this way?" In arriving at the answer ("No!"), we discussed the difficulties of arriving at an intuition of Elizabethan spoken English, but also considered some possible sources, including court transcripts and letters purporting to contain accounts of speech. We considered characteristics of Elizabethan spoken English from grammatical and stylistic points of view and also looked at resources for the classroom teacher seeking to overcome the language barrier felt by students. A primary resource is the 1988 NCTE publication by Randal Robinson entitled *Unlocking Shakespeare's Language.* In reaching beyond workbook paper/pencil activities, the classroom teacher also has classroom listening activities, video viewing, student acting, journal writing, and discussion all available as classroom approaches to the study of Shakespeare's language.

Notes

1. Rhymes, though, were not so far removed from Elizabethan society as they are today, with Muhammad Ali a singular pugilistic *and* poetic notable of the 1970s. Even Richard Day's 1578 *A Booke of Christian Prayers* has many brief poems directed to various social and occupational groups with *memento mori* ("remember death") themes in the margins of its pages. For those of us involved in print, this message is pertinent: "Leave setting thy page / Spent is thine age."

2. The reason a rate of 140 wpm is adequate for modern dictation, incidentally, is that the letter writer usually has many pauses, as well as many stock phrases, which enable the stenographer to keep up with the pace of dictation. Further, dictation usually is given only for a half hour or forty-five minutes at a stretch.

3. This color name, now lost to us, referred to a shade of red that was an imitation of a proper scarlet, a color associated with royalty. The *Oxford*

English Dictionary offers as one of its definitions of "bastard": "Having the appearance of, somewhat resembling; an inferior or less proper kind of." An example of this usage from 1670 is given: "a florid red, but paler than blood . . . resembling a bastard-scarlet."

4. The Star Chamber, the *camera stellata*, so known because of the gilt stars on the ceiling, was where the Privy Council met in Westminster for judicial deliberations.

4 Renaissance Books and Shakespeare's Use of Sources

Sometimes, when a class is working on grammar exercises, usually of the conjugation of past perfect or past progressive verb variety, or equally, verbals and their function in sentences, an intrepid student will say wearily, "Who invented English?" These same students are often gleeful at finding such "mistakes" in Shakespeare as, "This was the most unkindest cut of all." Shakespeare's larger mistakes (from a student point of view), his plotting excesses, are discussed in chapter 6.

The context of the student question about the invention of English provides a clear gloss on the meaning of "English." As a school subject, it means rules and grammar, bracketed from real-life usages and needs. As a taught subject, it may seem rule-bound, desk-bound, and teacher-centered to the student, something rigid and dull with no opportunities for genuine dialogue.

This chapter provides an answer to this question. It connects with chapter 2 on literary criticism in that it focuses on Renaissance books, especially on some of the ones relevant to an understanding of Shakespeare; these books, of course, help in the construction of the educational context in which Shakespeare wrote. Shakespeare wrote in an age before English grammar rules, copyright laws, and strict conventions governing plagiarism were developed. This fact helps to account both for some internal features of his drama as well as his publishing history in his own lifetime.

To answer this question, the teacher needs relevant facts from the history of the language, the history of printing, and the history of education in England.

History of the Language

Elizabethan English is early modern English. Some adults, educated adults, persist in referring to it—or even to nineteenth-century Dickensian English—as "old English." This it is not. Old English entails the period from 450 A.D. to 1150 A.D. and is known as a "period of full inflections." Middle English encompasses the period from 1150 A.D. to 1500 A.D., and is characterized as the "period of lost inflections." Just as even today we have regional variants of English, such as Southern dialect in America, so in the English Middle Ages there were regional dialects: Northern, East Midland, West Midland, Southern (Baugh 1978, 51–52, 189). Unlike the relationship between Southern American dialect and standard American written English, these dialects were less mutually intelligible. Of the four Middle English dialects, East Midland emerged as the dominant dialect for a combination of reasons: (1) it represented a middle between northern and southern extremes; (2) it was located in the most populous region of the country; (3) it was located in the same part of the country as the universities of Oxford and Cambridge (192–93).

Let us focus on population for a moment. London, located in the East Midland dialect region, had by the sixteenth century assuredly attained a position of social and economic preeminence in England. With a population of 250,000 in 1600 (Hirst 1986, 2), it matched or exceeded Continental cities of prominence. By 1640 it was the largest city in Europe. By way of contrast, Shakespeare's own Stratford, a thriving market town since the Middle Ages, had a population in 1564 of 1,200 to 1,400 (Schoenbaum 1977, 26). The late sixteenth-century cities in England nearest in population to London were Norwich, Bristol, and York, only one-fifteenth to one-twentieth the size (Coleman 1985, 68). London was the most common destination of those seeking betterment through migration (Morrill 1984, 294). Shakespeare's departure from Stratford for London some time after 1585 fits this category, as the chart on his annual earnings versus those of a schoolmaster[1] demonstrates (see p. 21). It seems odd to think of the life pattern of a genius as a sociological datum.

London's large population, the general fact of Tudor centralization of power and authority and specific instances of it, such as the outlawing of printing presses in such former printing centers as St. Albans, York, Tavistock, Abingdon, Ipswich, Worcester and their centralization in London and the two university towns (Slavin 1985, 136), all combine to make it inevitable that the dialect of Londoners would be the prestige dialect. But with the mention of Tudor restrictions on printing, we are getting ahead of our story, so to printing we now turn.

History of Printing

Before the invention of the printing press in 1455, manuscript books were prohibitively expensive for the ordinary person. A manuscript copy of the Bible took one year to make, and the ordinary priest could not afford to own a copy (Bishop 1970, 287). In the medieval period, monks saw writing as a form of manual labor which was pleasing service to God. Works which were copied on holy days of the church year were specifically enjoined from being sold for profit. In contrast to these monks who worked in scriptoria together, Torah copyists felt that only one copy of sacred scriptures should be produced at a time. They also followed an injunction in the Torah which stressed the copying of sacred scriptures on animal skin for greater durability (see Eisenstein 1979, 11–16, 59). The printing press, credited to Gutenberg in 1455, and humanistic philosophy, the inspirational breath of the Renaissance, effected far-reaching changes in these attitudes toward writing and in society at large, moving humanity in Western Europe away from a daily focus on the other world and toward a focus on the daily problems of this world.

In the early years after Gutenberg's invention, even royalty such as Richard III owned few books by today's standards. Richard, a man described as happiest when working, had a library of no more than six secular works (including a standard medieval work on warfare) in addition to some religious works (Seward 1983, 86). Only one commissioned illuminated manuscript was made for Richard—a treatise on war. Almost 150 years later, we see the Bodleian Library chaining its copy of the First Folio because of the cost of the book. By 1633, we also see Puritans complaining about spiritual cost, because reading the folios of Shakespeare and Jonson and other playwrights would take two years (see "William Prynne" in Campbell and Quinn 1966, 662–63).

Incidentally, early rare manuscript books are so costly now that some may constitute a sound investment for a union's pension fund. A ninth- or tenth-century Hebrew Bible, bought by the British Rail Pension Fund in 1978 for $286,000 "as an investment at a Switzerland sale," sold in December 1989 for $3.19 million ("Hebrew Bible," D14).

Books printed before 1501 are designated *incunabula*, a term indicating works issuing from the cradle period of print technology. England's great native printer in the fifteenth century, William Caxton, rocked the cradle in ways significant for our question, "Who invented English?" A successful businessperson originally from Kent, Caxton took up translating and printing as hobbies in his retirement as a way to avoid the idleness that he feared would give rise to the devil (Hindley 1979, 238). As Caxton succeeded in printing various works, including the works of Chaucer and Malory, for his customers, many of whom were wealthy nobles, he needed to make many language decisions about manuscript texts, especially concerning, in historian Geoffrey Hindley's words, "regional variations of English." Hindley reiterates the view that these printing decisions "have, rightly, given Caxton the reputation as the founder of modern standard English" (244). Caxton was "responsible for one of the truly significant events in the English social history of the fifteenth century," the "publication of the first printed book in England in 1477" (1). After Caxton, England had good Continental printers who established themselves in London. However, English printing techniques were not as advanced as the ones being developed on the Continent, and some displayed collections now show no English fine printing before the eighteenth century (G. Williams 1985, 67).

The Tudors, beginning with Henry VIII, were concerned with the usefulness of print to acts of political and religious subversion. It has already been noted that they restricted printing presses to London and to the two university towns of Oxford and Cambridge. The London Stationers under government approval controlled printing. Works were expected to pass approval of a censor and be registered in the Stationers' Register. Copyright regulations protecting authors' rights were not codified into law until the eighteenth century. "Pirated" manuscripts in Shakespeare's time were problematic for an author—profits and future printing rights belonged to the printer.

Books were advertised by bills posted in London; printers selling at St. Paul's and elsewhere had signs analogous to our modern day neon signs and copyrighted trademarks and logos. Hence, on the front page of Shakespeare's quartos, one sees the printer's name and usually his sign. *The Rape of Lucrece,* published by Richard Field in 1594, was found at the "Signe of the white Greyhound" in St. Paul's Churchyard; *Titus Andronicus,* published by John Danter in 1594, was available at the north door of St. Paul's at the "Sign of the Gun"; and Nathaniel Butter's 1608 botched *King Lear,* at the "Sign of the Pide [pied] Bull." One century earlier, Caxton's books were sold at the "sign of the Red Pale in the Almonry of Westminster Abbey" (Hindley 1979, 226).

People bought Shakespeare's quartos to allow themselves a more leisurely perusal of a work whose performance they had seen on stage and enjoyed. William Drummond of Hawthornden, a Scottish friend of Ben Jonson's, bought a *Romeo and Juliet* quarto for four pence in 1606 (in 1967, that quarto was worth 50,000 times Drummond's purchase price [Frye 1967, 91]).

History of Education

In the Middle Ages, monasteries and cathedrals had schools to train clergy. They also developed song schools or chantries to train young choristers to sing sacred offices. Guilds often had schools in their guildhalls. Instruction was heavily oral because often only the teacher had a copy of the text. Material had to be memorized. Printing brought about the presence of textbooks in the English classroom in the sixteenth century, but it did not immediately change the emphasis on oral teaching and pupil memorization.

In the late fifteenth century, schoolmasters sometimes developed their own school texts for their pupils. But the "To the Reader" in Lily's *Grammar,* a Latin grammar written for schoolchildren in the first quarter of the sixteenth century, makes it clear that Henry VIII sought a uniform—or at least uniformly orthodox—school outcome for the students in the 300 grammar schools he established in England:

> In the King's Majesty's wisdom he foresaw the inconvenience of
> Diversity of grammars and he provided the remedy.

The remedy was Lily's *Grammar.* By the time of Elizabeth, 10,000 copies of Lily's *Grammar* were sold annually in England. Schoolchildren such as Shakespeare had to know the entire book by memory (Campbell and Quinn 1966, 196). Did the King foresee that this book would remain a staple in English classrooms for 300 years?

The printing press as an education technology and the policy needs of Henry VIII and subsequent Tudors powerfully combined to shape, if not invent, English as a school discipline. Of course, Lily's *Grammar* was a Latin grammar. However, most of the textbook grammar studied in our schools even today is a Latin-based grammar, far better suited to Latin than to English, which is not even one of the Romance languages.

The school day for boys in Shakespeare's England began at 6:00 or 7:00 a.m., ran until 11:00 a.m., at which time were a lunch break and recess; school resumed at 1:00 p.m. and ran until 5:00 p.m. or 6:00 p.m. "This was six days a week, most weeks of the year" (Schoenbaum 1977, 67). In the petty school at age four or five, the child learned the alphabet, Nowell's *Catechism,* prayers, and handwriting. By age seven or eight, he was ready for the lower grammar school. Here he met Lily's *Grammar,* read moral maxims, moral poets, dialogues, and used the Geneva Bible to make his own Latin dictionary (67–69). In the upper grammar school, around age ten or eleven, the student practiced rhetoric and logic, while reading Ovid, Vergil, Horace, Juvenal, and

Caesar, among other authors, as well as being introduced to the Greek New Testament.

Did ordinary schoolchildren groan at this tyrannous regime? If so, their groans were inward probably, because of fear of the schoolmaster's prominently displayed rod. Several pictures of schoolmasters accompanied by rods or switches have survived from the sixteenth century. The faces in their classrooms look very sober. Although there were humane voices such as that of Richard Mulcaster, who advocated physical fitness as part of the school curriculum, and humanists from earlier in the century such as Sir Thomas More and from a little later Roger Asham, Queen Elizabeth's tutor, who believed in educating girls in languages and classical literature, there were also legendary whippers of the male students, including one about whom it was said by an unhappy boy that he warmed himself in the early morning English air by the vigorous motions used in whipping little scholars (see Henry Peacham qtd. in Nicoll 1957, 107).

What were the schoolchildren of the Renaissance like? Shakespeare's picture of the whining schoolboy in his Seven Ages of Man speech in *As You Like It* is well known. Less well known but delightful is the self-portrait which emerges in the Lisle letters in the correspondence of young James Basset to his mother.

The first point of interest for today's students is the separation of upper-class English schoolchildren from their families at a relatively early age. When James was only six or seven, he was placed with the Abbot of Reading while his family was living at Calais. At age ten, he wrote his mother in Calais from his school in Paris, the University of Paris. Today's middle-class culture's nuclear family has not been the norm in all times and places.

Second, students might enjoy knowing James's clothing requirements at age ten, at a school where a sort of uniform was worn:

> Apart from the regulation scholar's cassock of frieze cloth, worn by all students at Navarre, he is handsomely if soberly clad, in velvet, satin, taffeta, and camlet. Students were not supposed to wear ornaments on their headgear, but James manages to have two velvet bonnets, one of which is fashionably trimmed with gold buttons. His violet camlet gown is furred with marten, and he has a grey satin doublet. There is black velvet to make him a coat, and for guarding his cape and a doublet, and he has several pairs of hose with pullings-out of black and violet taffeta. A dozen shirts are made for him in his first year. He has cloth slippers and shoes of leather, and a trussing coffer in which to keep his clothes. (Byrne 1981, 323)

James wrote home at diverse times of his need for clothes.

Third, young James had definite ideas about his dietary needs, even during the fasting time of Lent. James's caretaker while he was in Paris wrote to Lady Lisle March 15, 1537, thanking her for sprats. He says "I shall have good use of them for your son, who cannot accustom himself to the eating of fish" (Byrne 1981, 318).

Fourth, while James was at the University of Paris, he felt, as many students before and since then have felt, mistreated by his teachers. He did not want to sleep with a servant and other boys in his room; reassurances had to be sent to his mother that the boys were "of great houses" and that the servant was a "gentleman's son" and a "clean-skinned" child (Byrne 1981, 324).

Finally, it may surprise students to realize that clergy livings could be assigned to one as young as James. At age eleven, by which time James knew both Latin and French, he was given minor orders and the living from an English prebend (i.e., the income from a church estate). A boy who found Lenten fasts taxing was, then, in charge of providing moral guidance for others.

James's opinionated young nature may well have caused the lack of endearment felt by family servant John Husee. Husee says—with rather thinly disguised sentiments of exasperation towards this mother's darling—that he thinks young James is better suited for the court than the clergy (Byrne 1981, 327). James did in fact end as a courtier, Gentleman of the Privy Chamber in the reign of Mary Tudor, and was married to Thomas More's granddaughter.

As a boy, Shakespeare was quite unlike young James Basset. Born in the countryside, the son of a glove maker, he attended the local grammar school, learning his lessons with all the others from Lily's *Grammar* and possibly from the rod. As a relief from the rigors of school, he enjoyed country sports, swimming without clothes on in a country stream, running over countryside fields, studying flowers and birds, May Days, religious feasts and holidays, mummings, morris dancing—the simple pleasures of country life. Any comparison of the folk traditions of the countryside with the lives and preoccupations of the privileged makes one wonder anew at those anti-Stratfordians who challenge Shakespeare's authorship of the plays. Kozintsev's vigorous refutation of a laced and powdered Shakespeare is glanced at in chapter 2. A fuller consideration of the motives and arguments of the anti-Stratfordians is given in chapter 5. I simply wonder, how could anyone think that someone from the class of James Bassett could have written Shakespeare?

The Author among His Books

What did Shakespeare's books look like? We will look at three types of books: a school book, a prayer book, a source book for a play.

School Books

Lily's *Grammar* is a Latin grammar. Explanatory parts are in English, as are the prefatory notes to the reader; the material studied and the exercises are in Latin.

Students and teachers who are accustomed to English grammar drills, especially the eight parts of speech, would take a natural interest in Lily's definitions of the parts of speech, some of which are close to our own, as is his definition of a noun:

> A noun is the name of a thing that may be seen, felt, heard, or understand [*sic*].

Others do not closely resemble our wording, even if they resemble our sense of the part of speech, as in this definition of an interjection:

> betokeneth a sodein passion of the minde, under an unperfect voice.

Because of the evident classifying spirit which lies behind this book, one can call to mind such comments as Juliet's to Romeo: "You kiss by th' book." This motif of the book-bound performer recurs very frequently in Shakespeare. (For other instances, see the clown catechizing Olivia in *Twelfth Night* or Touchstone's list of causes for quarrels in *As You Like It*.)

Students may be most interested in the graffiti on the Lily's *Grammar* I examined at the Folger Library. Done in brown ink, some graffiti resemble shields or suits of armor. There is a heart in the margin of one page, filled in with ink. In one place, the student user of the text has written, "Soft is my hand at my pene," and in a thankful effusion at the end of the book, "Finis amen." What student, or for that matter what teacher, in the month of May could not relate to the weary gratitude of this thankful brief prayer?

Prayer Books

Shakespeare was familiar with the catechism by Alexander Nowell. He may have known the prayer book by Richard Day, *A Booke of Christian Prayers*, published in London in 1578.

The prayer book is a beautiful book to look at and to hold. It contains many prayers for all the activities of the day, beginning with

prayers for rising, for dressing, and for going out. The book is heavily
and attractively illustrated, both in the margins around the prayers and
sometimes on the top or bottom of the page. It is replete with *memento
mori* instances, set down in rhyme. Death comes to many different
stations in life; though the words of the message vary according to the
station of the one called, the essential message is the same:

> Doctor divine at last
> Thy reading hour is past

or

> Preach no more about
> Thy glass is run out.

Some books that we take for granted in the classroom were not
available to Shakespeare as a young boy in the Stratford grammar
school. One is a speller. Richard Mulcaster's speller, first published in
1582, represents the most important sixteenth-century attempt to regularize spelling in English. In addition, it contained a list of 7,000
words in recommended spelling (Baugh 1978, 211). Though this list
was called a general table rather than our "spelling demons," it sounds
like a familiar teaching idea. Shakespeare was already out of school in
1582 and got married in November of that year.

Another work familiar to modern students, but missing from
Shakespeare's classroom, is a dictionary. Although Shakespeare and his
classmates used Latin words to construct their own Latin dictionaries,
they did not have an English dictionary to resort to. The first in English
was by Robert Cawdrey in 1604 (Baugh 1978, 231), *The Table Alpha-
beticall of Hard Words*, which defined 3,000 difficult words. By that year,
Shakespeare had already written three of the four tragedies this book
is focusing on. Only *Macbeth* still lay ahead.

Attitudes toward the vernacular were still being settled in the
sixteenth century. Scholars wrote in Latin, but translators made classics
of history, philosophy, and theology available to a wider reading public.
In fact, in Albert Baugh's view, the translators settled the Latin versus
vernacular debate by their practice rather than by abstract argument
(1978, 205). Baugh describes a delightfully vigorous provernacular view
exhibited earlier in the sixteenth century by Sir John Cheke in his
translation of St. Matthew's Gospel:

> where the Authorized Version reads *lunatic* he wrote *mooned*,
> and in the same way he said *toller* for *publican*, *hundreder* for
> *centurion*, *foresayer* for *prophet*, *byword* for *parable*, *freshman* for
> *proselyte*, *crossed* for *crucified*, *gainrising* for *resurrection*. (229)

The English language was in a state of fluidity in the late sixteenth century. Many words entered the language because of the printing press (Baugh 1978, 232). Shakespeare himself contributed to the expansion of the English vocabulary by his inclusive embrace of a vast diversity of words. Fortunately, our Stratford schoolboy never became a London Latinist.

Source Books

A 1632 print of an author in gown, hat, and ruff, seated at his writing table, shows him examining a book (reproduced in Frye 1967, plate no. 53). What does he see?

Many features of Renaissance books were different from the features we are accustomed to seeing in contemporary books. Features that we associate almost exclusively with textbooks or scholarly books, such as notes to the reader, were apparatuses in popular books as well.

The popular book on dueling by Vincentio Saviolo, *His Practise*, published in London in 1595, provided Shakespeare with Mercutio's dueling terms. When Shakespeare opened Saviolo's book, he saw these features:

1. a large-print dedication to the Earl of Essex;
2. notes to the reader, who is expected to amend the faults of the book;
3. few pictures, repeated throughout the book;
4. a single word typed at the bottom of each page below the other lines and repeated at the top of the next, to make copy collation easy;
5. a work cast in the form of a dialogue between a fencing master and a scholar: the master is supportive, while the scholar gives repeated thanks for instruction;
6. in addition to directions on fencing moves, an analysis of causes of quarreling, including mad-brained fellows, "froth of speech," the showing of weapons, suborning of servants, "marking" (i.e., staring at), the accusation of lying, and the just causes of avenging murder and rape.

Samples of quarrels observed by Saviolo are given, including one at a wedding or other ceremonial party in which a man asked a lady to dance without first asking leave of the men in whose company she was. The reader is counseled not to underestimate small men of the meaner sort. The author says, "Men do not come like woolen cloth, measured by the yard; those who think they may mince a man into pie meat may not." Throughout the text a link is forged between speech, honor, and the sword. Given this operative code, Romeo and Juliet did not have a chance.

Now imagine Shakespeare composing *Macbeth*. Many considerations are at hand: (1) he is a member of the leading acting company in the land; (2) he is writing a play for a performance before the King; (3) the King has a demonstrated interest in witchcraft, as evidenced by his book on witchcraft and his attendance at the trial of the North Berwick witches in Scotland; (4) others have used the King's interest in the words of spirits to entertain him on a visit to Oxford in 1605; (5) the English succession had been a pressing question throughout Elizabeth's reign. (Fraser links sixteenth-century, craggy-wild Scottish nobles and royalty with witchcraft and dark arts on numerous occasions [1969, 171, 198, 224, 229, 289, 302–03, 307, 369, 412]).

In John Leslie's book on Scotland, Shakespeare finds Latin text with marginal comments and gold leaf-edged pages. There is a foldout map of Scotland and a sinuous, rooted tree with blossoms on the tree, and shields suspended on branches trace James back to Banquo. In the upper left-hand corner, James is seated on armor resting on his crest, supported by rampant horses, with flags showing his coat of arms. In this genealogy, Shakespeare has an important source. Now for his story.

He finds the source he needs in Raphael Holinshed's *Chronicles*, two large books on the history of England, Scotland, and Ireland. He turns to the section on Scotland. First he sees the list of twelve authors "out of whome this Historie of Scotlande hath bene gathered," next the author's dedication to Robert Dudley, and then a helpful contents list before each chapter. He finds what he needs in the history of Macbeth and compresses background material before Macbeth's encounter with the women on the road. Yes, this encounter will grip the audience at court and the audience at the Globe alike.

Publication

Today we have a definite process in mind when we use the word "publication." The end point of the process is a printed text available to an anonymous reader in the home or school, or in a library or dentist's or physician's office, or on the subway, for private perusal. That good, effective writers do display a keen sense of their audience does not alter the reader's anonymity to the author. A shift in our outlook is evident in the fact that musical instruments were readily available in Elizabethan shops and taverns for waiting patrons (Garrett 1985, 229). Music, not only "the food of love," is public; reading is private, especially now, though in the past readers read aloud to themselves, read to others by the hearth at night for entertainment, and traveled in jobs as readers before the public.

In contrast to our definition of publication, in the Renaissance many writers did not publish their work through a printing press. Courtiers circulated works in manuscript at court. Many thought that of the genres we now consider creative writing, poetry alone was worthy of being printed. Shakespeare himself only had two narrative poems "cleanly printed, and it is not unlikely that Shakespeare was attentive to their publication and anxious that the poems should appear in decent dress. Such a statement can be made of none of the plays" (G. Williams 1985, 75).

Among popular writers the fiction was sometimes maintained that while the author of a work was out of town, the work was taken by a solicitous, nay oversolicitous, friend to a printer's for publication (Miller 1959, 141–44). This allowed the sheepish hack to escape the opprobrium of directly seeking publication. Nondramatic works which fared best in late Elizabethan England were utilitarian works, histories, religious works, alphabets, grammars, almanacs, and short, popular ballads.

Publication of plays meant dramatic performance at one of the public theatres, before the court, at a noble's house, or on the road during plague years. Shareholders in acting companies owned the rights to playscripts. To sell a script was to take away the advantage of novelty carefully guarded by the acting company. Scripts and costumes were among a company's most valued properties, as were its theatre building and inventory of props.

Shakespeare's plays were not printed until they were pirated. The piracies resulted from a confluence of causes: the plays' popularity at the theatre, the public's desire to reread the plays at leisure, a printer's desire for profit, a reporter's desire for profit, and perhaps the public's desire for entertainment in the event of the closing of the theatres in plague years. Once individual plays were stolen, Shakespeare and/or his company sought to have more accurate quartos available to the public.

The practice of pirating texts has made several kinds of information available to the forensic scholar. One, it is an index to tastes of the day. For example, *Romeo and Juliet* and *Hamlet* appeared in bad quartos, followed by good quartos, in Shakespeare's lifetime, whereas *Julius Caesar* and *Macbeth* did not appear in print until 1623. Several factors explain the popular appeal of the first two plays. The greater immediacy, personal applicability, and youth of the protagonists in *Romeo and Juliet* and *Hamlet* appealed to the consumers of the late 1590s and early years of the seventeenth century. By contrast, other, nontheatrical, more historically accurate information was available about both Caesar and Scottish history in the late 1590s and the first few decades of the seventeenth century, and had been available for some time. Further, I wonder whether James's response to *Macbeth* discouraged publication of it. Finally, I wonder whether the bawdy qualities of *Hamlet* and *Romeo and Juliet* detailed by Partridge gave these works greater appeal to an audience beset by Puritan sermons.

Second, the bad quarto of *Romeo and Juliet*, based on a visual recollection of the play, presents staging information by its stage directions. An example follows:

> At I.5.120 Capulet urges his masked guests to stay longer, but then at line 123, without explanation in Q2, changes his mind and bids them "good night." Q1, however, explains the change by the direction *They whisper in his ear* following line 121. (G. Evans 1984, 29)

This example is taken from the Cambridge edition. Numerous other stage directions from Q1 are listed in the Cambridge edition footnote on page 29 of its introductory material.

Plagiarism

Because plagiarism was not legally defined until the eighteenth century, today's strict textbook-defined standards did not obtain in the Renaissance. Additionally, the presence of—and the philosophy behind—the commonplace book would have made today's emphasis on originality very peculiar in the Renaissance (Ong 1971, 60). Why would an author even try to be "odd" in his conceits when the best that was thought was already available for his reflection and development?

Print was a relatively new technology even in Elizabethan England. Moreover, English printers were not as advanced in their formatting and cataloging techniques as printers on the Continent. By the layout of such books as Holinshed's *Chronicles* or Turberville's *Faulconrie* published in 1575, it is clear that authors garnered their books from flowers in the streams of thought available to them. Hence, we see in the early pages of Turberville:

> The names of those authors, from whom this collection of Falconrie[2] is borrowed and made, both Italians and French.

Miller makes clear that the best authors in the Renaissance were not the "scissors and paste" variety, which the hacks such as one Nixon were (Miller 1959, 210). Geoffrey Bullough, a careful student of Shakespeare's use of narrative and dramatic sources, has produced eight volumes on the topic. Obviously, Shakespeare used sources for plots, historical facts, and characterization. His artistry and theatrical sense frequently show in his omissions. In *Macbeth*, for example, he omits irrelevant, slow-moving background facts and also grossly violent episodes. He works toward the qualities that make drama compelling: tautness, compression, suspense, pacing, cumulative effects. At times, he is closer to his source than modern standards would allow. For example, in *Coriolanus*

> Shakespeare follows Plutarch so very closely that he often echoes the phraseology of the magnificent Elizabethan translation by Sir Thomas North. Volumnia's plea to her son in Act V, eloquently massive as it is, is scarcely more than a metrical adaptation of North's prose. (Levin 1969, 1212–13)

In general, though, Shakespeare's raw materials were changed in the furnace of his intellect into dramas of lasting interest and universal appeal. The Germans speak of "our Shakespeare" and claim to understand him better than the English. The Arab critic M. M. Badawi argued that Shakespeare was in fact an Arab whose real name was anglicized from Shayk al-Subair (Paolucci 1985, 675). We do not find such claims for writers like Holinshed, Sir Thomas North or Saviolo.

Teacher checkpoint. In this chapter we visited late medieval and Tudor classrooms. We sat on oak benches and paid special attention to the kinds of books used by Elizabethan schoolmasters and their pupils. We also looked at the author seated at a desk and perusing the wares of the booksellers in St. Paul's.

In doing so, we have now situated Shakespeare in his speech and writing community. In the next chapter, we will situate the author Shakespeare, this time not in his study, nor in countryside market town Stratford or crowded London in detail, but as he is known to us and to our students in the classroom.

Notes

1. Schoenbaum considers the theatre tradition (recorded by the antiquary John Aubrey from the words of the actor William Beeston) that Shakespeare was a schoolmaster before turning to drama to be a possibility, though not a certainty (1977, 110–11).

2. Spelling variations persisted in the late sixteenth century. Baugh states that "our spelling in its modern form had been practically established by about 1650" (1978, 213). Hence, in earlier texts we might encounter variant spellings of one word within the same text.

5 Shakespeare, Biography, and Challenges to Authorship

A teacher addressing an open house audience of parents of social studies fifth graders was praising the class and giving examples of their collective brightness. She told how in their animated discussion of Columbus's discovery of America, the class asked such questions as, "Did they just see the land when they set foot on it on October 12, or did they see it before then?" Her response to these students was characteristic of many overworked, frazzled teachers: "I don't know. Let's get on with the lesson. Anyway, it doesn't matter." Every teacher and every lecturer has had to say "I don't know" at some point or other. Also, every teacher likes to both move the lesson forward and to feel competent by being on the grounds of his or her expertise. So, many times there is both a place and a necessity for the second statement, too. However, the teacher's final statement may represent too quick an attempt to reach closure. And it may represent an effort to bypass the one real opportunity for learning.

The biography of Shakespeare is full of such open questions as "Was his date of birth April 23, 24, or 25?" In fact, part of learning in many areas consists in learning to live with plurality and uncertainty as well as in learning the consequences of choosing one view rather than another. Chronology is extremely important in biographies, history, textual studies, and histories of ideas. Two scholars who are especially skillful at a kind of mathematical, or case-by-case, consideration of the implications of documentary evidence are Schoenbaum and Leeds Barroll. Barroll's careful documentary study of the connection between the Saturday, February 7, 1601, performance of *Richard II* and the Earl of Essex's uprising which began the next morning throws considerable doubt on the facile interpretation that drama is subversive. To take another example, such ideas as the doctrine of equivocation[1] look entirely different if they are conceptualized as being coolly, rationally arrived at in the spacious, sunny warmth of the Spanish library at Valladolid in the 1560s, as is erroneously maintained by Frank Huntley (1964, 391) than they do if we visualize them as arising in the context of the English persecutions of recusants of the 1580s and 1590s. (See Malloch 1966, 145 for the date of 1584 as the earliest source of textual antecedents for the doctrine; this date comes after the execution in 1581 of Edmund Campion.) This doctrine is not only relevant to *Macbeth* and to *Hamlet*, but also bears on Juliet's deception of her mother over the cause of her inconsolability and Antony's deception of the conspirators as to his intentions in his funeral oration.

Two questions loom large in student minds when they think about Shakespeare's biography. One is whether he was, in fact, the author of the plays; students wonder because they have heard speculation suggesting that Shakespeare could not have been the author; also, students may have seen the PBS special broadcast on the topic. The other question students are curious about is whether Shakespeare was gay. Again, they have either heard this from another teacher, or they have noticed the dedications for the nondramatic narrative poems or misread a sonnet or two. Or possibly, they have noticed the earring Shakespeare sports in the Chandos portrait (reproduced in Campbell and Quinn 1966, 654).

This chapter will build answers to these questions; in addition, it will briefly consider the latest form authorship attacks have begun to take.

What have we got on which to build Shakespeare's biography? Bones, houses, a little handwriting (signatures and hand D^2 on a few pages of a play on the life of Sir Thomas More), church and legal documents, and portraits. What's missing? Isn't this all we have from anybody? The thing that we're missing is the personal side—a diary, a manuscript of one of his plays in his own handwriting, statements about his literary philosophy and methods, letters to his wife, statements from neighbors, expanded statements from fellow authors (not formal poetic tributes from Ben Jonson, but real, off-the-cuff remarks), reminiscences by mistresses, "tell all's" by his two daughters—in short, the author with all the warts and quirks that we are familiar with from contemporary standards of biography. Writing from the dry documents that are available is somewhat like trying to construct a picture of a modern man from his ChemLawn bill and its envelope with the cool, green diagonal lines and lush green drop of grass on the return address (such a bill leads to a portrait of a man who is "a green thought in a green shade").

Because the somewhat sparse details of Shakespeare's life are widely and readily available, I will not summarize them here. However, I would like to summarize some interesting questions raised by the careful documentary approach taken by Schoenbaum in his *Compact Documentary Life* of Shakespeare:

1. the faith in which Shakespeare was raised;

2. the number of years Shakespeare attended the local grammar school;

3. the willingness or unwillingness Shakespeare had in getting married and his feelings afterward;

4. whether Shakespeare was once a heavy drinker under a crab tree, as the legend states;

5. whether Shakespeare poached deer from Sir Thomas Lucy's deer park, as the legend states;

6. whether Shakespeare acted in the countryside, saw the Kenilworth pageant honoring Queen Elizabeth in 1575, or saw mystery plays at Conventry (which were performed until the suppression in 1580);

7. whether Shakespeare was a schoolmaster in the countryside (likewise, later, was he ever a legal clerk, soldier, sailor, printer, barber-surgeon, physician, "what you will" [110]);

8. why Shakespeare left Stratford;

9. why Shakespeare's father's prosperity as well as his prominence in town civic affairs seemed to decline.

Almost every one of these questions has some bearing on our reading of Shakespeare's plays. For example, at one point or another, critical debate has raged over whether King Hamlet's ghost is Protestant or Catholic and over whether Shylock's forcible baptism reserves him for a Christian heaven. The question of what faith Shakespeare was raised in would possibly help supply an answer, although it would also be necessary to know Shakespeare's adult attitude toward that faith—hostile, warm, still faithful, indifferent, or selectively committed. In addition, Schoenbaum treats other questions that arise from the early years in London:

10. the dates of Shakespeare's first works;

11. what acting company Shakespeare was associated with first;

12. what Shakespeare did during the plague years; for example, whether he traveled to Italy (this question is discussed in chapter 6).

When discussing these questions in class, teachers should help students to see how different answers lead to different interpretations of intentions in the plays, but should allow them to draw their own conclusions about what kinds of biographical information about Shakespeare would be helpful in understanding his works. Interestingly, Alfred Harbage echoes one of Shakespeare's admirers, Charles Dickens, in feeling a sense of relief that so little is known: "The actual records, as I have said, preserve a neutrality which seems almost a calculated gift of destiny" (1966, 20). I concur, but others might not.

For students with a creative bent, the circumstances of Shakespeare's marriage—to a woman eight years his senior who was three months pregnant—can lead to all kinds of stories of "black-eyed wenches," secret meetings in the sylvan forest of Arden, moments of stolen passion, dramatic revelations of consequences, feared parents, and elopement in a cold and dreary November. Another source for stories is Shakespeare's early career in the theatre, first as horse holder for nobles and gentlemen at the theatre, and only a short while later, as a playwright, fighting off splenetic attacks in print by Robert Greene, Cambridge wit.

Given the kind of plausible information that is available about the man Shakespeare, some students may never even have entertained the sentiments of the anti-Stratfordians and may wonder how and why they have come about. One way to introduce the topic is to show students Max Beerbohm's cartoon from his series of literary caricatures, "William Shakespeare, His Method of Work" (1977, 69). The drawing shows a smiling Shakespeare tiptoeing away from a scowling Francis Bacon, who is surreptitiously handing Shakespeare a scroll entitled *Hamlet.*

Among the four baker's dozens or so of individual claimants or syndicates who have been proposed for the authorship of Shakespeare, some of whom seem more plausible than others, are: Christopher Marlowe, a dramatist; Francis Bacon, England's great philosopher and prose writer; and the Earl of Oxford, a minor amateur poet and a wealthy man.

Notes for a Reply to the Anti-Stratfordians

Those looking for a succinct scholarly summary of the arguments about Shakespeare's authorship should examine the Folger booklet by James G. McManaway. In what follows, I give my own arguments in the hope of making the discussion accessible to both teachers and students.

Shakespeare had no college degree. That's akin to saying Steve Jobs couldn't be the inventor of Apple computers because he didn't go to college. In a new field, one not yet crushed under the weight of bureaucracy and laws, the enterprising, energetic, insightful, talented, and lucky individual has a large scope for his or her ability. Also, consider writers much later than Shakespeare who had neither a college degree nor even a high school education—this describes Charles Dickens some 200-plus years after Shakespeare's death.

Also, consider the nature of an Elizabethan grammar school education. The point has been made by many scholars that the supposed "small Latin" that could be acquired there exceeds that of all but a few of our university-trained students today. Also, consider the nature of an Oxford B.A. in the sixteenth century. As a research project, students can investigate how many Oxford-trained clergy, physicians, and lawyers wrote plays or poetry. They might also examine the quality of the literary writing. Miller's book on writing as a profession in the Renaissance suggests that a number of the university-educated writers were financially struggling hacks.

Shakespeare was too educated. Shakespeare's supposedly prodigious learning may in reality reflect our lack of the same learning, a Latin- and classics-based learning. It may well be true that Shakespeare remembered far more of what he learned in school than the typical pupil did then or since. It is also quite possible that Shakespeare trained himself to skim sources for specific purposes. As for his knowledge of foreign cities and traditions, many of us have learned about other places through conversations with travelers.

Also, on the topic of Shakespeare's desire for learning generally and his technical knowledge of such fields of the day as law and medicine, we all know lay people who fancy themselves experts in these fields and who in truth have mastered some jargon and some interesting case histories. Additionally, we all have known people who were not well-educated by the degree standards of our day but who nonetheless like to read and learn (our "philosophers at large" by night, discussed on page 105).

Shakespeare knew how royalty spoke. It is prominently said by anti-Stratfordians that Shakespeare includes many scenes with royalty and that he, as a country-bred person, could not have known how royalty would speak. My reply to this follows:

1. Queen Elizabeth made public appearances and remarks which were widely circulated in Elizabethan England.

2. Shakespeare himself was in a royally sponsored company after 1604. At times his company performed before Elizabeth's court, and four times as many performances were done before James's court.

3. Chapter 3 indicates how difficult it is to develop an intuition

of Elizabethan spoken language. It also shows highly placed Thomas Cromwell speaking repetitively and blusteringly; likewise for Henry VIII himself. Since Shakespeare wrote poetic dramas, how do his critics know that Elizabethan royalty and courtiers *did* speak this way?

4. The amateur effusions of such courtiers as Walter Raleigh are much more limited in their interest than the work of the noncourtier, Shakespeare. Perhaps we have the truest portrait of a young courtier in the foppish Osric sent to Hamlet in Act V and the truest portrait of a senior statesman in Polonius.

5. What about the speech of our own "royalty"? Richard Nixon's Watergate tapes, Ronald Reagan's spontaneous remarks, George Bush's—are they brilliant rhetorical jewels? What about our own school administrators—are their extemporaneous or written remarks memorable?

6. Mark Twain complains about routine rhetorical excess in Shakespeare. This catches the anti-Stratfordians in a contradiction. If all of the characters' speech is excessive, then the speech of royalty cannot be an accurate imitation.

Shakespeare's signature was messy. Anti-Stratfordians who have studied Shakespeare's signatures pronounce them illegible and him an unlettered ignoramus. This ignores the fact that the script of the day, English secretary hand, is not like ours and can only be read fluently by paleographers or other trained people. Incidentally, some of the features of standard written English are the result of gradual accretions in the direction of standardization wrought by our print culture. Queen Elizabeth's letters were not punctuated according to modern standards. If we judged our own doctors by their illegible handwriting, what pronouncement would the anti-Stratfordians make about their intelligence and fitness to practice medicine?

There are no autographed copies of the plays. This is a modern complaint based on the literary collection habits of our day. It is premised on a failure to recognize the effects of uniformity in schools, public life, and modern record keeping; the cult of the individual (wherein parents save a lot of their children's school and childhood memorabilia); and the orientation of our day toward the collection of art as well as artifacts for profit. People who bring up this point have not invested themselves in the facts of the late sixteenth and early seventeenth centuries in England. Those who lament that little is known about Shakespeare are perhaps unaware of the fact that no birth date is known for Spenser, nor is there any poetry in his handwriting. Spenser, recall, was a highly regarded poet in his day and eventually became a feed poet laureate of the nation. Likewise, no birth date is known for Raleigh, nor are there handwritten pages of his book of history, written in the Tower. Virtually nothing is known of Webster, and even Ben Jonson has "lost years." However, more is known about both Jonson and Marlowe than the others because of their aggressive personalities (McManaway 1962, 4–8).

We have no folio from Shakespeare's lifetime. Consider the attitudes toward publishing in Shakespeare's time. Power and profits lay with the stationer and publisher, not the author. Also, consider the attitudes of the time held by acting companies toward their playscripts. For Shakespeare to have voluntarily sought publication for his plays as they were appearing in repertory at the theatre, or to have published a collected volume in his own lifetime, would have undercut his own company. The playscripts were a company's carefully guarded possession—its edge over a rival acting company in box office competition. In a way, the scripts were analogous to the carefully guarded recipes of the medieval guilds, secrets at the heart of their mystery.

Make a comparison to the classroom. Most teachers do not make voluntary videotapes of their classroom performances for posterity or even for the present. Many teachers do not share the written details of their best ideas with fellow teachers. Also, the fact that our culture values entertainment, both in sports and in performing arts and media, far more than it values teaching, and hence the fact that we teachers leave little trace in movies or record books, does not stop us from trying to do a good job in the theatre of the classroom.

Shakespeare had only a minor role in the acting company. In a time when acting and theatres were targets of Privy Council directives and Puritan attacks and most actors and entertainers did not prosper, Shakespeare belonged to the premier acting company in the country. The fact that tradition assigns to Shakespeare the playing of minor acting roles in his company, combined with his personal financial success as shown in the documents detailing his real estate purchases, argues strongly on behalf of the conclusion that he was the writer for a company in which he was an actor-shareholder.

To sum up, what seems to drive the anti-Stratfordians is a combination of anti-elitism (intellectually) and elitism (socially and economically). At heart is the feeling that it cannot be true that one person could have written such great drama and acquired such a huge following with sheer creative genius. The basis of the argument is that no individual from a small town could have written these dramas; only a wealthy person would have the education, taste, and leisure to do such work. This view elevates money and privilege over intellectual ability. It also concretely ignores the love of clothing, sports, court life, and falconry among many of the wealthy. All these interests took intellectual energy and time as well as money to maintain.

————

The more recent attacks on authorship do not concern themselves with biographical details. They either state frankly that works are determined by material culture (Dollimore and Sinfield 1985, viii) and hence cannot be universal, or they say that a work is a product of language and ideas of the time and hence should not be attributed to one author. The former view is mainly the message of Marxists whose political views have been challenged in the theatre of the world by the events of 1989 in Eastern Europe. The latter view seems to consist of what Robert Coles calls the "envy of the storyteller" (qtd. in Allen 1990, 90); it also entails an ideological position that could deny individual responsibility, hence undermining an important aspect of our Western legal system.

These views put these intellectuals in interesting company. For example, the Puritans who eventually closed the theatres in the 1640s had been working their agenda through sermons before the ultimate revolutionary actions of the 1640s. In their sermons they preached against idleness, drunkenness, fornication, and generally against the countryside culture of maypoles and dancing, with its potential for sedition (Hirst 1986, 76). In this soil, fanaticism could flourish. For example, fanatical Sabbatarianism led to a jury finding a butcher not guilty of murder "during a Sunday football match" because the victim died "by divine visitation" (76). I wonder if deconstruction extremists would say that authors do not compose or "own" their writing because they write by cultural visitation. As people who have sweated it out over blank white sheets of paper will readily say, they only wish it could come by this method.

One useful aspect of these new intellectual attitudes is illustrated in the provocative title of the essay by Alan Sinfield: "Give an account of Shakespeare and education, showing why you think they are effective and what you have appreciated about them. Support your comments with precise references" (Dollimore and Sinfield 1985, 134–57). However, this title (a spoof of a British pre-university exam topic) makes a sweeping assumption about the motives and behavior of British schoolteachers. Some of us, British and American, don't follow this indoctrination approach anyway.[3] I hope those looking for new approaches to teaching the sundry students we see in our classrooms will find some ways of engaging students in chapter 7 and elsewhere in this book.

Finally, teachers who wish to address student curiosity about whether Shakespeare was homosexual should make sure students know about literary conventions of the Renaissance which might lead the modern reader—perhaps mistakenly—to assume that Shakespeare was homosexual. The practice of dedicating works to wealthy patrons in hopes of financial gain was widespread in the Renaissance, as was the vigorous expression given to male friendship found in the sonnets. In the absence of extraliterary evidence, the assertion that Shakespeare was homosexual is unprovable and seems likely to remain so.

———————

Teacher checkpoint. Facts about Shakespeare's life are available in many places, including our literature anthologies. In this chapter, we've explored biographical questions which arise in the study of Shakespeare's life, and we have seen how those facts have importance to students studying Shakespeare's plays. We have looked in particular at challenges to Shakespeare's authorship of the plays, including a newer, more intellectually exotic challenge. We have briefly glanced at the claim which is sometimes made that Shakespeare was homosexual, and have questioned the evidence for the claim.

Notes

1. Based on the Aristotelian concept of propositional truth, especially with regard to mixed propositions (i.e., verbal/mental, verbal/written, written/mental), equivocation as practiced by fugitive Jesuits in England in the late Elizabethan and early Jacobean periods consisted of giving answers whose aim was to elude magistrates attempting to catch and convict priests and recusant Catholics (i.e., those who dissented from the newly established state religion). The use of equivocation was to be limited to matters pertaining to religion and the practice of religious faith as a response to the Tudor imposition of a state religion. According to John Gerard, it could not "be invoked in ordinary conversation to the prejudice of plain truth and Christian sincerity" (Gerard, 1951, 126). It was a technical, trial-oriented strategy of evasion.

2. Hand D is a specimen of handwriting in Elizabethan English secretary hand consisting of some lines of dramatic verse inserted in the text of the play entitled *The Book of Sir Thomas More* submitted to the Master of Revels for official play approval. The text contains seven different handwritings, including the censor's. Hand D is thought to be Shakespeare's. The reader may review the paleographic, thematic, and stylistic evidence in Schoenbaum (1977, 214–17).

3. Sinfield believes that the secondary examination system, determined by boards controlled by single universities or combinations, specifies the intellectual and emotional direction the student being examined is required to take in his or her written essay. Sinfield especially accuses the current uses of Shakespeare as being complicit in the "construction of gender and sexuality." A cultural materialist, he would like to see the teaching of Shakespeare's plays "bring down capitalism" but complains that this is "unlikely" (Dollimore and Sinfield 1985, 154).

6 Shakespearean Plotting: Dramatic Conventions and the Elizabethan Context

Our literature anthology textbooks frequently put questions after each act of a play. This format unfortunately breaks up the flow of the action of the play. For students reading *Romeo and Juliet* for the first time, it also gives rise to a sense of startlement when they begin reading Act II. This is reflected in the question: "They've just met at this party and they are planning to get married???" Students sometimes thumb the pages of their books to see if they have missed some scenes, some passage of time.

"Knowledge begins in wonder," said Aristotle. This special moment of wonder can be seized on by the alert teacher to address several kinds of questions: (1) If students were writing *Romeo and Juliet*, what scenes would they insert between the Capulet party and the balcony scene? Let them try their hand at dialogue and then stage what they have written. Do the results make theatre as interesting as theatre which assumes and shows a boundless love and its consequences? (2) Consider the Renaissance audience. They were not children, but adults. Our teens need and want to see how it's possible to know whether somebody in their lives is Mr. or Ms. Right. This was not the concern of an audience at a tragedy. Besides, by 1597, Shakespeare had already written comedies showing people falling in love and love's confusions. Playbills advertising a play were posted in town. By its nature, a love tragedy assumes two people suddenly—and in spite of obstacles—in love. (3) Consider the reaction of the Oxford undergraduate readers of the play. For young people looking forward to an arranged marriage, the balcony scenes in this play were compelling and satisfying as they were. (4) The source—a narrative poem—does show a longer time span (Whitaker 1953, 110). Shakespeare takes three months from the source and turns it into four days. Yet drama does not by its nature allow the same kind of introspection and leisurely development as narrative, a form our students are more familiar with from short stories and novels. Soliloquies, according to Globe Theatre expert Bernard Beckerman, are usually either emotive, cerebral ("philosophical comments, plotting, and moralizations"), or invocative, and thus are not interior psychological probing by modern standards (1962, 184), but were directed outward by the actor in performance. However, supposing soliloquies can give more of a glimpse of interiority than other forms of dialogue in Renaissance drama, note that Shakespeare has supplied his audience with a more intense form of soliloquy in the balcony scene: Romeo speaks of his beloved as he looks at her in hiding; Juliet then speaks, unaware that she is being overheard by anything but the stars in the night; then they speak together.

Drama requires continual display: unfolding, change, development. The pace of drama engages the audience in an intense way. It engages readers, too. This is why I have been stressing reader response as an appropriate classroom literary critical framework since chapter 2. The image of life in drama is more like the speeded-up biology presented in time-lapse photography than it is like the actual growth of a bean seedling over the course of two weeks. By contrast, the more leisurely format and very different audience of the novel allows for a slower development, which perhaps met its apex in the loose and baggy monsters of the Victorian period—or the subtle, interior-oriented novels of Henry James.

In drama, there is no time to describe a scene, apart from a character describing a scene. (The exception, of course, is the figure of Time in *The Winter's Tale*, but this is a special case, not the general case.) Other fundamental requirements of drama are surprise, pressure, and energy. By surprise I mean that the audience can be familiar with the story, but the staged performance still needs to contain something different in the staging to keep the audience interested. Also, collaterally, the audience must not be allowed to become so jaded and blasé that it surrenders the illusion of the drama. Ten-year-olds watching a Christmas parade might giggle and poke each other, saying knowingly about Santa, "I see where his beard is fastened on at the side," but a theatre audience is supposed to be engaged. They can wonder, but they lose the pleasure if they are as knowing as these sage boys. Drama must contain an irreducible residue of magic. With drama, we

> . . . take upon's the mystery of things
> As if we were God's spies. . . .
>
> (*King Lear*, V.ii.16–17)

Another element of drama is pressure. Characters pressure each other by what they say. When the words become particularly interiorized by one character, the pressure builds up and translates into action.

Hamlet's father's words create an interior pressure in Hamlet that drives him forward. In the audience, this pressure becomes a feeling of tension: What will happen? How, when, and where will the pressure be released? The audience already knows or senses the "who" and the "why," and this induces in the audience a state of tension until the total release occurs. A drama could scarcely be written about an entire cast of stage characters who feel no pressure. One Bartleby in literature is enough, one Brick in *Cat on a Hot Tin Roof* is enough, and two of these in a classroom is a recipe for frustration. Because this pressure is so important, it seems wrong to ask questions such as "What is Hamlet doing while Polonius's family talks together in the middle of Act I?" At that time, there is no Hamlet for the audience. The audience is expected to focus on Polonius's family and vicariously experience whatever pressure they are feeling from their interaction.

The third necessary feature of drama, one consequent upon that building pressure, is energy. The characters must be capable of doing something and must act in some fashion. Consider both Romeo and Hamlet. By Act II, scene ii, the lovesick Romeo has not simply sighed to Benvolio; he has also intercepted a party invitation, talked to Mercutio, crashed a party, danced with and talked to Juliet, fallen in love, hidden from Mercutio and Benvolio, and leapt over an orchard wall. Hamlet, who according to Olivier, his best twentieth-century interpreter, and many other university-ensconced hesitators, cannot make up his mind. Still, he not only talks to a ghost, but he dismisses Ophelia to a nunnery, commissions a play and writes lines for it, talks to his mother in her closet, kills Polonius, boards a pirate ship, forges a commission to the King of England, jumps into Ophelia's grave to argue with Laertes, and duels with Laertes. No wonder he is scant of breath by Act V. His actions are hardly quiescent. In fact, energy displayed or released as action was a vital part of theatre in the open air, done for audiences of 3,000. A lot of image hunting and allusion hunting done in the scholar's study ignores what we can learn more obviously from our own popular entertainment. Dynamo Tina Turner said in an interview that her music dictated her costumes, and not the other way around. She started out in formal, expensive gowns but tore them or fell in them. Then she started wearing short skirts. The excesses of violence of *Titus Andronicus* represent Shakespearean plot in a formal gown; but his plots worked toward short skirts, too.

This discussion has brought us to a two-headed coin which certain critics skip in scornful dismissal at drama in general and perhaps at Shakespeare in particular. On the one hand is the anti-theatrical prejudice felt by some twentieth-century Continental critics. It seems clear that the reason for this prejudice is their own critical agenda, which is both to abolish the significance of texts and to deny the authority of authors over their works (see Pease 1990, 112); for further discussion of this point, see chapter 5. Drama, with its power to enact, display, and engage emotions, would be particularly annoying to such critics. A story of passion and of suffering causes the audience to feel emotions, to feel wounded and healed, as Weimann says (1985, 276), not just to feel engaged in a cerebral game of wordplay. Further, Shakespeare's worldwide acclaim makes him a particular target of deferred delight to the deconstructionists.

The other side of the criticism directed against Shakespeare, most strongly by such prominent figures as Voltaire and Tolstoy, is the unclassical nature of his plots, which seem such a stout ragout when judged by the thin-sauce classical unities of both Greek and seventeenth-century French drama—time, place, and action. Shakespeare's texturizing of scenes and acts by mixtures and contrasts could in some world not awed by his reputation make him fare ill at the hands of judging English teachers and their students, tutored by the textbook canons of simplicity, clarity, and coherence, as well as grammatical correctness and avoidance of clichés and plagiarism. The spirit of his works would no doubt garner some marginal red marks from zealous graders.

It is far from my intent to side with Robert Heilman's comment that Shakespeare is "now beyond judgment" (qtd. in Veidemanis 1964, 247). This is hardly a useful approach in the classroom. In fact, in the remainder of this chapter, I would like to examine certain plot features which puzzle contemporary students, either as being downright wrong, or at least anomalous. The plot features can best be understood in the social and political context of the Renaissance, as well as in light of certain aspects of the Elizabethan stage.

Treason

Political treason is a central concern of *Julius Caesar, Hamlet,* and *Macbeth.* The Roman plays, of which *Julius Caesar* is one and *Coriolanus* another, have an interesting stage history of suppression and/or audience disturbance in various places because of their possible subversion of an actual ruler. *Julius Caesar,* for example, was banned in Russia after the French Revolution and was not allowed to be performed throughout nineteenth-century czarist Russia until 1897 (Speaight 1973, 112). A stage performance of *Coriolanus* in 1934 in France "caused serious riots, as both Communists and Fascists considered it to be a deliberate affront to their political notions" (Harrison 1955, jacket notes). Both Russia and France have histories of political oppression; audience sensitivities are, or were, sharpened in the circumstances outlined above. By contrast, American school students, raised in a democracy, have only a dim consciousness of political assassinations. Despite press horror stories about our students' total ahistoricity, I think they do know about Lincoln, though probably very little about McKinley, or about Garfield, the circumstances of whose death—at the hands of an office-seeker— hardly qualify him for this discussion.

In the sixteenth century, in a more controlled society, treason had a broader application than it does today. A wife who killed her husband committed a treasonous act. Parliamentarian Peter Wentworth challenged Elizabeth in 1576 on free speech in Parliament and was sent to the Tower (J. Levine 1969, 136); Puritan John Stubbs made the mistake of meddling in Elizabeth's courtship by the Duke of Alençon. When he "libelously suggested that the Duke of Alençon was 'unmanlike, un-prince-like,' un-English and was interested in an elderly English heiress solely because of the size of her royal patrimony" (Smith 1975, 71), he had his right hand removed for this offense. Because there was a strong presumption of guilt behind a trial at the King's Bench, the passersby who questioned the guilt of an underling being hanged for the Overbury murder were "arraigned . . . *in camera stellata*" (White 1967, 117–18) for disturbing government process.

Although regicide was debated in the antigovernment writings of Jesuits and of Calvinists on the Continent, regicide was widely regarded as a grave crime. In addition to the perceived threat of regicide in England, two French monarchs were assassinated in the space of less than twenty-five years, Henry III in 1589 and Henry IV in 1610. In Holland, William of Orange (William I) was struck down in 1584. In all these cases, the assailant was religiously motivated, thus demonstrating to a twentieth-century American audience accustomed to random violence the inflamed religious climate of the late sixteenth and early seventeenth centuries.

Spying

Rosencrantz and Guildenstern are employed by King Claudius to spy on Hamlet. Later on they are meant to be the instruments of his death. Macbeth says of the noble houses which surround his uneasy reign:

there's not a one of them but in his house
I keep a servant fee'd.

(III.iv.131–32)

Elizabeth Tudor's reign was marked in part by plots to install a Catholic ruler on the throne and restore the Old Faith in the country at large. Some plots bear the marks of the hand of the government as instigator, in order to further the aim of winning popular sentiment for harsher repressive measures against Catholics in the country. Those who defend Elizabeth would point to the Papal Bull of 1570, excommunicating Elizabeth and excusing English Catholics from the duty of obeying their sovereign, as creating a situation necessitating the use of spies. Further, Elizabeth's defenders would point to the presence in the country from the 1580s onward of the Society of Jesus, an organization of Catholic priests whose presence Elizabeth outlawed in 1585 and two of whose Spanish members—Juan de Mariana in 1599 and Francisco Suarez in 1613—were to write brilliant defenses of regicide. Spies and double agents were most certainly used to track down such Jesuits as William Weston and John Gerard, who have left us their autobiographies; in Appendix J to John Gerard's book are descriptions of the priest by Richard Topcliffe and others, made available to Elizabethan hunters of recusants, whose position was equivalent to our Wild West bounty hunters.

The plots most familiar to the reader will be the broad outlines of those swirling around Mary, Queen of Scots, kept under arrest in England from her entry into the country in 1568 until her trial and execution in 1587 after the discovery of the latest plot, and the failed enterprise of the Spanish Armada in 1588, apparently finally triggered by Mary's death. Sir Francis Walsingham, Elizabeth's secretary of state, is said to have been the first of the modern state administrators to fully realize the potential of the state for spying and the utility to the state of having spies (see Fraser 1969, 541). The London dramatist Christopher Marlowe, who died in a tavern brawl by the sword thrust of an agent provocateur, is thought to have been in Walsingham's employ on the Continent. Another Walsingham employee, Dr. John Dee, was listed as agent 007 (Hussey 1978, 19), a prototype of our James Bond. Among Elizabeth's spies on the Continent were those engaged in drawing maps of rivers, towns, and fortifications in the Netherlands (Martin and Parker 1988, illus. 19); others had infiltrated the ranks of the Armada planners to as far a level as they could (126–27) but could not reach to Philip II's inner circle.

Just as Hamlet intercepted and counteracted the charge against him being carried by Rosencrantz and Guildenstern, those plotted against by the Elizabethan government occasionally developed their own strategies in return. Several Jesuits imprisoned in the Tower have reported in their autobiographies how they sent secret messages from their cells: William Weston wrote in the juice of marigold flowers—he chewed a dry, withered flower he found in his cell to make an ink (1955, 93); John Gerard wrote in orange juice (1951, 119) and, of course, eventually effected his escape in a daring nighttime plan—the only person ever to successfully escape from the Tower.

While we moderns adopt a stance against police entrapment (consider the reportorial brouhaha over the F.B.I. luring a drug dealer to Lafayette Park, across from the White House, so that President Bush could, in a nationally televised speech, show a bag of cocaine sold so close to the White House), the Elizabethans most assuredly did not. Their attitudes and practices contain fertile material for student short stories and playlets; in this context, Hamlet's plot against the plotters should be completely unsurprising:

> There's letters sealed, and my two schoolfellows,
> Whom I trust as I will adders fanged,
> They bear the mandate; they must sweep my way
> And marshal me to knavery. Let it work.
> For 'tis the sport to have the enginer
> Hoist with his own petar, and 't shall go hard
> But I will delve one yard below their mines
> And blow them at the moon. O, 'tis most sweet
> When in one line two crafts directly meet.
>
> (III.iv.203–11)

Censorship

In *Hamlet*, the following exchange takes place between King Claudius and Hamlet when the play within the play is almost concluded:

> *King:* Have you heard the argument?
> Is there no offense in't?
> *Hamlet:* No, no, they do but jest, poison in
> jest; no offense i'th'world.
>
> (III.ii.224–27)

The King is suddenly asking Hamlet whether the play has passed the censor's approval. In this case, rather oddly, he is asking Hamlet, his "mighty opposite."

Novelist Graham Greene has described the surface of Shakespeare's plays as "smooth and ambiguous" (1951, xi). Shakespeare has been described as our most impersonal writer; drama itself is an impersonal medium. These features, which may be perceived as puzzling objectivity on the part of the dramatist, may be accounted for in part by the censorship of Shakespeare's time.

The Lisle letters, a collection of letters written by and to Lord Lisle and his family members, contain ample evidence of the perceived need for caution in speech and writing in the period they cover, 1533–1540. This period saw Henry VIII switch marriage partners almost as fast as we used to switch Twist partners on the dance floor. The switches had legal sanction. In 1534 an Act for the Succession "made it high treason maliciously to deny or attack the Anne Boleyn marriage" (Byrne 1981, 74). Even in 1547 when the King was visibly declining, it was "high treason to prophesy the King's death" (Hibbert 1971, 65).

Queen Elizabeth imposed restrictions on court speech pertaining to her marriage possibilities (see J. Levine 1969, 108), on entertainment via a strengthened office of Master of Revels, and on certain books. In 1599, for example, books by Thomas Nashe and Gabriel Harvey were burned "in Elizabeth's greatest bonfire of books" (Miller 1959, 191) for deviation in matters of religious doctrine and for challenges to the government. Tudor ecclesiastical courts, presided over by the local vicar, heard offenses which included swearing. Punishments for some conduct offenses could be public and humiliating. Some offenders were required to make public confession at Sunday church services (Brinkworth 1972, 15).

Today school newspapers pass the approval of a school censor. But adult magazines do not. In fact, many magazines print material which the editorial staff might in some way disagree with, if one can judge from the disavowals of responsibility or agreement printed on the masthead page of some magazines.

Even in our country some types of speech are restricted; these include the kind of irresponsible, potentially hurtful speech encompassed by "crying fire in a crowded theatre," jokes about assassinating the president or other civil officials, and jokes about hijacking aircraft. Freedom of speech and speech-symbolic acts does extend to burning the flag. Currently, challenges are being raised about the kind of art the government should sponsor. One case which raised this concern was the exhibition of Robert Mapplethorpe's photographs on display at the Contemporary Arts Center in Cincinnati, Ohio. The major legal question is whether taxpayers' money can be spent on art objectionable to some taxpayers. The Elizabethan answer is an unequivocal "No." However, even the Elizabethans tempered the interest of some members of their society in exerting complete control over artistic expression. Yet, although Elizabeth protected the theatres from Puritan assaults, both by legislation and by requiring acting companies to keep in practice by their public performances so as to be able to give private performances for "the Queen's solace," at no time did the Globe company's income from performances before the Queen total more than 5 percent of their revenue (Beckerman 1962, 22). Incidentally, the proportion of the King's Men's income from James eventually grew to 15 percent.

Melancholy

There is some evidence of melancholy, or brooding, in Romeo, Hamlet, and Cassius. Romeo's is the result of neglected love; Polonius believes Hamlet's is from the same cause; Cassius, clearly, is a political malcontent. From 1566, two years after Shakespeare was born, comes the story that Robert Dudley, spurned by Queen Elizabeth, locked himself in his room in a melancholy state of dejection for four days (J. Levine 1969, 46). In our modern, nonmonarchical era of easily available birth control and relaxed attitudes towards sexual promiscuity, it would be very hard to find an equivalent to such elaborately postured behavior. Since our society seems to abound in cases of spurned lovers turned maniacal killers, it is doubly difficult to find an equivalent for students to relate to.

To understand Hamlet's and Cassius's melancholy, which was of the political sort, might require a look into the writings of Machiavelli, with his classic advice to political seekers on how they are supposed to behave in cases of lagging fortunes. Cassius, surveying the ground of expectation with a careful eye and being ever ready for the right opportunity and showing a willingness to use whatever means will succeed, is a model Machiavellian—while Hamlet with his tortured conscience is far from it.

Interestingly for Hamlet—and for Macbeth, too, who seems too vigorously warlike to be a sufferer from melancholy—the Renaissance cure for melancholy, according to Timothy Bright, "doctor of physic," is wholesome air, thin and pure—not "marrish, misty, foggy air." (Now we know the cause of all that brooding in movie versions of Poe.) In diet, the melancholic should avoid beef and venison, taking younger meats instead, as well as fowl and certain types of fish (fast-moving fish, not slow fish from deep, murky waters). The dwelling place of the patient should be cheerful and of a middle level, neither too low nor too high. Clothing should be light in color, not black or dark. When Hamlet's mother tells him "cast thy nighted color off," she is giving advice consistent with the medical advice of the day. In some cases bloodletting may be necessary. Finally, sweet music is restorative, since the mind, according to Aristophanes, is a kind of harmony. Yet many of our students seem to find solace in distinctly unsweet music. This course of treatment prescribed by Bright helps combat the effects of the source of melancholy, i.e., oppressive vapors rising towards the brain from the abdomen.

Fighting

Elizabethan drama was violent and passionate. The tradition of Senecan drama, calling for blood, verbal thundering, and continual chambers of horrors, required stage violence and passion. The reader who is interested in Senecan revenge elements in *Hamlet* can explore this topic further in books such as Bullough's which study sources.

Unintentional violence occasionally occurred in the theatre building itself. Shakespeare's biographer Schoenbaum relates the incident of a stunt where an actor was tied to a pillar where he was supposed to be shot; instead, a pregnant woman and a child in the audience were killed (1977, 146). An episode which Shakespeare surely eventually heard about involved the first husband of the wife of John Heminges, of Shakespeare's acting company. The man was slain in a duel while on tour near Stratford (117). Another episode which Shakespeare must have known of was Ben Jonson's imprisonment for killing actor Gabriel Spenser in a duel in the fields at Shoreditch. Jonson seems to have had a humor disorder himself.

The bear-baiting arena near the Globe was bloody and violent, though accepted in Elizabethan times; the Queen herself even liked the sport. Star bears included Harry Hunks, Sackerson, and Tom of Lincoln (Carter 1973, 27). In this context we recall Macbeth's final, grim, animal-like courage:

> They have tied me to a stake. I cannot fly,
> But bear-like I must fight the course.
>
> (V.vii.1–2)

The Elizabethan theatre used animal blood and entrails on stage:

> They staged scenes of execution in which the entrails of animals bought from the slaughterhouses were plucked out from the "victims" and exhibited to the spectators, as was done in earnest at the hanging, drawing and quartering of victims by the executioner at Tyburn. (Hodges 1973, 74)

Elizabethan executions of religious dissidents were so violent and public that a Dutch artist produced a grim reminder in *Theatrum Crudeletatum;*

this and other notice on the Continent caused an outcry which made Elizabeth somewhat abate the ferocity of the executions.

Vincentio Saviolo, whose book on dueling appeared in London in 1595, listed the causes of fighting he had observed. These causes are included in a discussion of the format and sample contents of a Renaissance book in chapter 4.

The territorial markings and appropriation of colors and shoes as exclusive gang symbols in Los Angeles may not seem to some to represent cultivated or admirable behavior, but they are not unprecedented historically, either. When the Earl of Surrey, known to English teachers as the Surrey of Wyatt and Surrey sonnet fame, wanted to make sure that everyone recognized his claim to Henry VIII's throne by having the royal lions painted on his coat of arms, he was executed by Henry (Hibbert 1971, 60). Similarly, Mary, Queen of Scots, and her husband Francis rather haplessly fashioned themselves rulers of England as well as Scotland and France (Fraser 1969, 97–98).

The marketplace fighting in Verona seems so sudden and unexpected. However, Saviolo reports fighting caused by so little an offense as one person "marking" (i.e., staring at) another. Sometimes children's quarrels break out over one child staring at another. Likewise, Hamlet's fighting with Laertes at Ophelia's funeral seems bizarre, until we read in Roland Frye that fighting in or around church grounds was common in the sixteenth century, because this area was "the common meeting place for the whole community." Also, fights over funeral precedence, a sign of social status, sometimes postponed the burial of an important person for as much as a month, or even erupted in violence in the funeral procession itself. One man jumped into a grave to arrest a corpse for debt (1984, 248–49, 353).

Poisoning

Poisoning enters into the stories of both Romeo and Hamlet in rather fantastical garb. First, Juliet is given a potion from Friar Laurence which will induce in her a deathlike state for forty-two hours; among her fears before taking the drug is the possibility that it is actually a poison. Later Romeo does buy a poison from a lean, impoverished, law-breaking apothecary. In *Hamlet*, the prince's father died from having a poison poured into his ears, which at once caused his skin to be covered over with a bark-like crust. Students accustomed to modern medicines find these circumstances implausible. One student perceptively commented on the fairy-tale quality of Juliet's potion, which reminded her of "So Snow White ate the apple. . . ."

But poison was a common murder weapon in the sixteenth century. According to the *Hamlet* source study by Bullough, the Duke of Urbino did in fact die from a poison poured in his ear in 1538 by a barber-surgeon bribed by the Duke's enemies (1973, 32). If you are curious about Italian Renaissance revenge, read Bullough to find out how the Duke's son punished the luckless barber-surgeon. Closer to Shakespeare's own time, when Mary, Queen of Scots's husband was sick with an ear infection which traveled to his brain, a condition unrecognized by the medicine of the time, it was suspected that "an Orleans barber had poured poison into his ear, while doing his hair" (Fraser 1969, 122). Many fears of poisoning dominated the reigns of Mary, Queen of Scots, and Queen Elizabeth. In fact, the Jesuits were even accused of such purely fantastical plot hatching as attempting to poison Elizabeth's saddle pommel "with a sticky mercurial preparation which she would take on her hands and so into her food" (Edwards 1985, 23).

"Green men" and "green women" were countryside herb gatherers who were known to Londoners, too. Just after the completion of Shakespeare's playwriting career, two sensational episodes almost stranger than fiction unfolded in the Tower. The first was the systematic murder by poison in 1613 of Sir Thomas Overbury by Frances Howard, Countess of Somerset, for fear of his opposition to her marriage to Robert Carr. The reader can see page 51 for an inventory of the pharmaceuticals she used, some of which she received from country herbalists.

The second episode centers on Sir Walter Raleigh. Stephen Greenblatt stresses the artful in Raleigh's execution: his use of nonfatal ointments and emetics which induced a disease-like state in him, not far from King Hamlet's leprous crust, in an attempt to postpone his beheading (1973, 4). This gave Raleigh four days' time in which to write out statements which he hoped would stave off his execution. As it happens, he was beheaded anyway.

Pirates

When Hamlet is taken by pirates before he is two days at sea, it may appear to students unacquainted with the Renaissance that this plot twist resembles the work of Snoopy at the typewriter writing his great novel, with its mixture of a shot ringing out, the maid screaming, and a pirate ship appearing on the horizon. However, throughout the 1580s and 1590s, English pirates were busy harrying and raiding Spanish ships and Spanish cities such as Cádiz. The waters around Spain, the Azores, and the Spanish possessions in the New World, especially in the Caribbean, were full of ships headed by the likes of Sir Francis Hawkins, Sir Francis Drake, and Martin Frobisher, all eager to get what plunder they could for themselves as well as for the crown. In fact, Walter Raleigh's harrying of Spanish towns in the New World along the Orinoco River on his last expedition there is what finally led to his execution during the administration of James I, who was more pro-Spanish than Elizabeth had been.

Family Units

Students accustomed to the family units they see on *The Cosby Show* or *Full House* do not understand the family and household groupings in Shakespeare. In particular, my students have found Juliet's isolation as well as the identity of the Nurse and her servant Peter puzzling. Some sociology of the Elizabethan family is helpful.

For many families, the nuclear family was the rule, consisting of a household of 4.5 members in the seventeenth century (Hirst 1986, 23). However, this rule did not apply to nobles and gentry. The Capulets and Montagues were prominent families. *Macbeth, Hamlet,* and *Julius Caesar* center on royalty or rulers. The households are much larger than a contemporary middle-class readership can relate to: students who live in large extended families will more readily understand these households.

In an age of arranged marriages, Juliet's desire to choose for herself may well represent Shakespeare's own country experience in marrying at age eighteen a woman of his choice, eight years his senior. For royal marriages, royalty would view portraits and listen to ambassadors' reports on prospective marriage partners. In fact, Henry VIII's disappointment at the actual appearance of his fourth wife, Anne of Cleves, led to the downfall of Thomas Cromwell, Henry's advisor. Marriage partners sometimes had a wide disparity of ages, as did the Capulet partners themselves. There were child marriages and pregnancies—and consequently deaths, remarriages, and wardships of defenseless, unprotected children. If the goal of arranged marriages was to improve one's family's social and economic standing, the goal of those who trafficked in wards was to make money from the sale of wardships and their wards' lands and marriageability; the goal of the Master of Wards was to supplement his income from government service (in actuality, the office of Master of Wards was one of Lord Burghley's main sources of income [Stone 1967, 192]). An important element in maintaining social order in the seventeenth century was the key role of the father, in his household and as head of his apprentices and servants (Hirst 1986, 50). Perhaps the masterless person was feared as some fear the homeless today. Hence, Juliet's defiance of her father was a threat to the social order. Lord Capulet's response seems monstrous to contemporary teenaged readers. But stories are preserved of the physical abuse directed toward Lady Jane Grey, England's queen for nine days after the death of Edward VI, by her own parents. Likewise, Sir Edward Coke, revered in English legal history as the father of common law, was abusive toward his daughter.

Juliet, who for all the Italianate veneer seems an English girl, would not have attended school, as there were no schools for females in Elizabethan England. Though companions for royalty's nurseries had been carefully chosen during the reign of Henry VIII, and both Henry's daughters and those of Sir Thomas More were very well educated, a girl such as Juliet would have learned needlework, dancing, playing a musical instrument, and perhaps she would have learned to read well enough to read the Bible. It may also have been important to Juliet's parents for her to learn to run a household (see Grafton 1985, 61). It is by no means assured that Juliet would have known how to read. By mid–seventeenth century, England had a female literacy rate of 10 percent, in contrast to a 33 percent literacy rate for the adult male population. This broad average would vary according to whether one were talking of country or city people, and according to their occupations. "Townsmen were around two-thirds literate" (Hirst 1986, 20).

Juliet's only companion seems to be the Nurse. Often poor relations—single women—were hired at the houses of gentry as companions to the females and teachers of needlework, and also out of a sense of charity.

Commoners

Shakespeare himself was a commoner until his father, with Shakespeare's help, secured for himself the crest of a gentleman and the permission to sign himself as such. Shakespeare saw in the city of London not just commoners from the country like himself, come to the city to make their families' fortunes, but a city of variety and activity, alive with the cries of vendors, bustling with coaches and merchants, full of taverns, swindlers, masterless people, people going to sea, apprentices to gold-, silver-, and tinsmiths, tailors, as well as nobles in elegant clothes, citizens and citizens' wives—and he delighted in listening to the talk of all, not just the wealthy. Servants in prosperous households "borrowed" their social rank from their masters. This is evident in the argument between the Capulet and Montague servants, as well as in the livery or cloth worn by servants to indicate who their employers were (Stone 1967, 102). Another category of person kept in the noble household is the clown. The clowns in the gravediggers' scene in *Hamlet*, like the porter in *Macbeth*, grew out of the role of the medieval clown, who was suffered to speak on matters involving social criticism (Weimann 1978, 11–14). The gravedigger in *Hamlet* is designated as Clown, from Q2. Some critics, including Voltaire, disliked Shakespeare's habit of mixing clowns and kings in the same scene. But Henry VIII had a court jester, Will Somer; Elizabeth's jester was Richard Tarlton. In Shakespeare, a license to speak is granted to clowns; sometimes it is granted to female characters disguised as men.

Traveling

Students can look at the distance from Verona to Mantua on a map of Italy. The small-scale map can be deceptive to the modern student accustomed to cars and inexpensive American gasoline. The main point to note is the variability of traveling in the Renaissance:

> In the sixteenth century a journey between the same two points could take days, weeks or months, depending on the weather, the state of the roads and bridges, the availability and mode of transport, and the presence or absence of bandits. (Martin and Parker 1988, 180)

To these conditions may be added the presence or absence of plague in a town. Plague prevents Friar John from getting through to Romeo with word of Friar Laurence's plan. A total of 11,000 died in London between December 1592 and December 1593 (Schoenbaum 1979, 93); in fact some scholars speculate that Shakespeare traveled in Italy at this time. In *Hamlet*, images of disease and death abound. *Macbeth*, too, depicts Scotland as sick.

Suddenness

Shakespearean timing is often compressed, if not downright abrupt. One boy who was puzzling over a true-or-false question on Friar Laurence's potion—"The potion's effects last 72 hours"—said to me,

"I couldn't really remember, but I knew too much would happen in a Shakespeare play for it to last that long." Bright student; keen insight. Romeo and Juliet meet at a party, fall in love, and are ready to get married and/or die for each other in less than a night and a following morning; Hamlet's alteration toward his mother, Claudius, and Ophelia indeed follows a wild and whirling course throughout the play; Macbeth is no sooner made thane of Cawdor than he is seen to be contemplating murder, his wife is seen to be reading his letter, and he is seen to be seeing daggers and committing murder offstage.

Drama is not a novel; only significant events are shown, and most mental activity cannot be portrayed. Further, there is an emphasis in the disparate literature of the late Elizabethan period on suddenness, from Vincentio Saviolo's listing of some causes of quarreling in his book on dueling, to King James's book on some actions of witches. The age was abundantly aware of *memento mori*, not just in art and prayer but in life; the *carpe diem* poems flourished in this awareness in the seventeenth century. Also, one should note Shakespeare's change of his sources. In Holinshed, Shakespeare's source for *Macbeth*, for example, the actual historical period chronicled spans a much longer time than does the play; Macbeth "reigned justly for ten years before he attempted to murder Banquo and Fleance" (Whitaker 1953, 286). Drama is a mirror of life, but an altering mirror, by the nature of the genre. Likewise, the sources for *Romeo and Juliet*, *Hamlet*, and *Julius Caesar* all are compressed in the fire of Shakespeare's theatrical imagination.

Some incidents seem so sudden as to be unwarranted. One example is the reporting of Romeo's mother's death. We can say that Shakespeare's artistry was not yet as mature as it was in *Hamlet*, when Ophelia's death is not only reported but rendered in memorable lyric by Gertrude. However, the nature of Romeo's mother's death—death by grief—is not so farfetched. Sir Christopher Hatton was "said to have died of chagrin" when Elizabeth "became tired of him" (Creighton 1893, 143); many a one has died from a stronger, more forceful, and sudden cause then and since.

The Supernatural

Juliet fears to see Tybalt's ghost; Hamlet and Brutus actually see ghosts. Macbeth sees witches and ghosts. The sixteenth century had literature on prodigies, ghosts, and witches, written by "doctors of physic" and by King James alike. In his *Demonology*, besides giving proof of the existence of witches, the King considered the rudiments of their magic—

words, herbs, stones, circles, and conjurations—and their powers: they can make men or women love or hate each other, can lay sickness upon people, can bewitch or take the life of men or women by "rosting of pictures" (waxen pictures), can raise storms and tempests in the air which are "soudaine, violent, and short induring," can make folks become frantic or maniac, and can make spirits follow or trouble persons or haunt houses. Those of infirm and weak faith are most prone to the power of witches. This would seem to describe Macbeth. Lest it be thought that only the King and the ignorant believed in witchcraft, at Frances Somerset's poisoning trial, testimony brought to light Lady Frances's dabbling in occult practices: "a figure in which was written this word Corpus, and upon the parchment was fastened a little piece of the skin of a man" (White 1967, 122). Also, when Tower guards attempted to put Frances in the cell in the Tower where she had systematically poisoned Sir Thomas Overbury, she exclaimed: "Put me not in there; his ghost will haunt me!" (qtd. in Hibbert 1971, 92). For dramatic emphasis Frances shrieked and fainted.

John Gerard records a number of mysterious occurrences. One woman reported a mysterious light in her bedroom after the death of her husband; another reported a mysterious knocking on the door after the death of her husband. After the brutal execution of Father Oldcorne, his intestines were said to burn for sixteen days after his death, even in rain; finally, the straw beneath the scaffold where Father Garnet was executed showed a kind of image of his face (1951, 38–39, 179, 202, 274–76). Available evidence suggests an active interest in ghosts and evil spirits by Protestants and Catholics alike (Frye 1984, 17–18). In fact, it was rumored that when Edward VI died, Henry VIII's tomb cracked open to show Henry's displeasure at the loss and at England's succession problem (Smith 1975, 43).

Whether Shakespeare himself subscribed to these beliefs is rather beside the point. What he realized is that the phenomena of ghosts and witches made compelling theatre, and he used ghosts and witches as characters in his plays.

Globe Theatre

Theatre architecture of the day led to playwriting in which fluidity, special effects, and scenes painted in language were all characteristics. Charney finds in Shakespeare's plays an extensive use of contrasts and a wide range of emotional and declamatory effects. We are, by contrast, encouraged by our schools and society at large to approach problems rationally and neutrally and to keep a tight rein on our emotions.

Plot Architecture

The Aristotelian view of drama frequently taught in school is linear in its depiction of rising and falling action. Elsewhere I have noted Professor Hammersmith's objections to the imposition of the Aristotelian framework on Shakespeare. The conventions of some of the genres popular today, such as situation comedies and detective shows, may be fitted to this Greek model, with its exposition/complication and rising action/climax/resolution/denouement. In Shakespearean tragedy, a linear model can be set aside in favor of a topological model. Topologists study such exotic shapes as Klein bottles and Möbius strips.[1] They also study knots. In my view, the Shakespeare plot runs along on several tracks or threads, which become hopelessly knotted at the turning point; after this there can be no happy solution. Because the thread is soft and moveable, rather than rigid like a line on a graph, there can be a continuing rise in the intensity felt by the audience even after the technical turning point.

———————

Teacher checkpoint. In this chapter, we've used our mental map of Elizabethan England—and sometimes the physical maps supplied by such Elizabethans as Christopher Saxton and John Stow, and Continental engravers George Braun and Claes Visscher, as well as our own contemporary interpreters such as C. Walter Hodges—to visit places like some of those we visited in chapter 3. Our on-site locations in London included the Tower, the court, the bear-baiting arena at Paris Garden, and crowded London streets. We even went on the high seas with the English sea dogs in search of Spanish gold.

We looked at these locations with two ideas in mind: (1) drama is different from novels or expository writing; (2) when Shakespearean plotting is examined in its historical context, such seemingly archaic or foreign plot devices as the introduction of pirates seem appropriate.

Note

1. Klein bottles and Möbius strips are one-sided surfaces named after German mathematicians.

7 Shakespeare in the Contemporary American English Classroom

My African American students sometimes wonder where they fit in with a "white writer, a white man" such as Shakespeare. Also, the children of the newer American immigrants and their teachers may well wonder how they will negotiate their encounter with such a strongly established canonical author as Shakespeare.

In chapter 2 I review the newer modes of criticism which came so strongly to the fore in the 1980s. Many are actually varieties of reader-response criticism, a way of reading which emphasizes the reader's affective response to literature, not just a predetermined cognitive response. Given the diversity in our student population and the fact that even in a fairly homogeneous class student reactions to literature can be quite varied, reader-response theory leads to a practical approach which teachers find constructive and helpful in the classroom. This chapter begins with some statistics on the new immigrants, the human beings, we see in our classrooms every day. Then, we explore teacher attitudes which are compatible with a reader-response classroom. Finally, suggestions are made for making connections between students and Shakespeare via the bridge of reader response.

The New Immigrants

New immigrants have been coming to the United States since the 1960s. Previous waves of immigrants have had racial, cultural, and linguistic features in some ways more complementary with those of the citizens of their new land. Predominantly from European cultures, many spoke languages with Latin roots and languages which use the Roman alphabet. Of the new immigrants, many of those from the Caribbean, Latin America, and the Philippines speak Spanish. Their language has these roots and this alphabet. But for many others, especially those Asians from Cambodia, Laos, and Thailand, their languages have little in common with English. The Hmong, moreover, have only been writing their language for thirty years. In our own hemisphere, Haitians who speak Creole have been writing their language for only fifty years

(Kellogg 1988, 202). Population growth rates of the new groups contrast in striking ways with those of already established U.S. groups. The following figures taken from Kellogg suggest that these growth rates will have a strong impact on U.S. public schools:

	average children per lifetime
European Americans	1.7
African Americans	2.4
Mexican Americans	2.9
Hmong	11.9
Cambodians	7.4
Laotians	4.6
Vietnamese	3.4

Kellogg notes that because of migration settlement patterns, half the U.S. population growth "since the 1980 Census has occurred in just three states: California, Texas, and Florida" (202). By the year 2000, more than half the California student population will consist of children of non-European descent (204).

Implications, Teacher Assumptions

Each child exists in the world in a body. Drama is meant to be acted with bodies. One assumption the teacher should keep in mind throughout this chapter is that with the New Critical approach to Shakespeare's plays, we began taking the "body" of the words when we should have been taking their spirit to breathe into and be enfleshed in our bodies. A colleague who attended a summer seminar for secondary teachers in Stratford mentioned that the seminar director referred to English teachers as "people of the page" whereas the performance-oriented are "people of the stage." Who knows more about what it feels like to be Juliet: the married English teacher who met her spouse at college, or the new student from India whose parents still practice the social custom of arranged marriages? Who better understands the lived inner struggle of Brutus: the drama teacher who voted for Ronald Reagan in 1980 and 1984, or the new student whose parents fled a dictator's land in Eastern Europe? Many such students can teach us and their classmates from more comfortable backgrounds much about what they have seen and how they have lived.

Charney notes that German audiences in the 1590s who saw Elizabethan traveling companies in Germany during English plague years were thrilled by the performances they saw, even though they did not understand English. Charney stresses the "significant language of gesture and stage properties which communicates meaning to us" (1961, 8). This is the second important assumption for the teacher to keep in mind as this chapter develops. Students who know no English can still enjoy a dramatic performance of Shakespeare. This is different, of course, from image hunting in a text.

The third assumption is that minority readers' reactions to canonical literature may not be the same as the teacher's rhapsodic appreciation or rather fixed, unchallenged view of the text's meaning. Minority readers' reactions may make the teacher uncomfortable. Consider the statement by James Baldwin, who said he discovered in Shakespeare's bawdiness the

> ineffable force which the body contains, which Americans have mostly lost, which I had experienced only among Negroes, and of which I had been taught to be ashamed. (qtd. in Paolucci 1985, 676)

A Nigerian editor of *The Tempest*, Michael J. C. Echeruo, poignantly stated that the new readers of Shakespeare's play have

> not only new interpretations based on the experience of a new set of readers, but cruel deductions arising from the evidence which the play offers of prejudices and attitudes meant originally only for true English ears. (qtd. in Paolucci 1985, 673)

Echeruo goes on to say that writers of African descent relate to Caliban in looking at the world's Mirandas. The likelihood that Shakespeare wrote "originally only for true English ears" is indeed great. Consider the numerical relevance of a statistic taken from another context, an interview with director Joseph Papp: "There were only perhaps seven hundred Africans in England in Shakespeare's time, and very few Jews" (Gallo 1988, 16). However, I don't think Shakespeare was intolerant in his outlook. Rather, Shakespeare expressed a sense of wonder and admiration for things novel, rare, and strange, as can be seen in Romeo's exotic tribute to the marvel of Juliet set like a gem in the familiar surroundings of Verona in the evening:

> It seems she hangs upon the cheek of night
> As a rich jewel in an Ethiop's ear—
>
> (I.v.45–46)

We can help students find these passages of celebration of things rare and marvelous.

Our students' attitudes are neither so fixed nor so articulate as

Baldwin's or Echeruo's quoted above. Here is where our own attitudes
are important. We can always work with and emphasize the strength
of our students' responses. This is assumption four. My African American
students, for example, can read *Romeo and Juliet* with sly humor, seeing
a double meaning, for example, in Capulet's dirge:

> All things that we ordained festival
> Turn from their office to black funeral—

(IV.v.84–85)

One boy said, "Uh-oh, call Peterson and Williams" (a local black-owned
funeral home). In fact, their humor, their love of language, and their
passionate responses to the theatre on the page and in the classroom
are part of the positive energy of my school day. Moreover, when I
took a field trip as a parent-chaperone to Tuskegee in February two
years ago as part of Black History Month, I became more aware of the
connectedness between Booker T. Washington's philosophy and many
Renaissance attitudes. Booker T. Washington taught his students about
the signs of God in nature, and he spoke in an oratorical tradition.
George Washington Carver shared with the Elizabethans an interest in
extracting dyes from nature's plants. Teacher Kathleen Ross has written
affirmingly of her experiences in teaching humanities to students assumed by school officials to be low achievers; she also reports being
dismayed with teachers who told these students that they shouldn't
waste their time with things they can never understand (1989, 48). This
attitude guarantees the results which are too often produced in those
teachers' classrooms.

Harsh and exclusive-minded critics such as John Simon do not
make the teaching task any easier for teachers trying to cultivate both
skills and attitudes in their minority students. Simon argues against
interracial casting of Shakespeare's plays, unless a distinctive group
such as all the fairies in *Midsummer Night's Dream* are cast black. And
Simon goes further. He basically wants racial casting done according
to the racial makeup in Shakespeare's time, i.e., fair-skinned Anglo-
Saxons. Further, he wants pronunciations done by old spelling standards,
e.g., "porpentine" rather than a modernized "porcupine" in *Hamlet*,
and preferably the greater "musicality" of an altogether British cast,
whose language, he says, has "a melody—that the American language,
a much flatter and unmelodious thing, lacks" (1985, 868). It is good
for a debater that Simon is an extremist; this makes demolition easier.
The conclusions Simon reaches would seem to say that Shakespeare is
not universal, but race and island-nation bound; thus, there is no reason

for anyone but the British to bother about him at all, including Yugoslavian-born John Simon living in New York City. Hence, we've come to our fifth assumption, perhaps the most important one of all—really, the one my readers have been assuming all along. Shakespeare is worth teaching because he concerns himself with universal values which find expression in all cultures, no matter the differences in skin color, eye shape, or speech accent.

To acquaint all students with Shakespeare is to acquaint them with an important English writer. Not to do so is part of an insidious pattern of regarding some students as being forever culturally and linguistically outsiders. Knowledge of Shakespeare is valuable for its own sake; seeing his plays gives both emotional and aesthetic pleasure. All our children have a right to know the best of our great writers and to make their own judgments. Bill Moyers speaks of a group of plumbers in Utah who wrote to him about their developing an "addiction" to philosophy after viewing his PBS program, *Six Great Ideas.* They said: "We may be plumbers by day but at night we are philosophers-at-large." Moyers's response: "I don't know how our nation will survive unless every citizen becomes a philosopher-at-large" (Filteau 1990, 6). I don't know how we as English teachers could justify not making the effort to teach Shakespeare to all our students.

The final assumption is that there are other ways of defining "minority" than the usual racial or ethnic designations assumed in the preceding paragraphs. One way is by sex. Women were the "second sex" in Shakespeare's time. Though they were important in the domestic economy of England and though they enjoyed emotional intimacy with their spouses, they could not own land without special permission, their subservience was stressed, and they often came into their own as persons only as widows (Hirst 1986, 17–18). Printers' widows, for example, sometimes continued to own and operate their deceased husbands' shops. Whether women are still regarded as the "second sex"—and the relevance of this question to the classroom—will vary somewhat from one class and teacher to another.

The word "minority" may have its most interesting application to yet another group, those people with unusual or unpopular points of view. Peter Milward, for example, who has written several books on Shakespeare and the Bible—from the point of view of a believing Christian—recognizes that he is swimming against a critical tide which he says "may well be called one-sided in its rigid secularity" (1987, viii). Or, to take another example, Peter Levi says of his negative reading of the characters of Elizabeth's main advisors, the Cecils, that it is part of his being "unwilling to accept the established, establishment view of Elizabethan England." He also says, "The image of Shakespeare as an honorary insider, the national poet of a golden or heroic age of English history, is overdue for demolition" (1988, xxi). Finally, Carolly Erickson's criticism of the Queen herself makes Erickson a distinct minority among Elizabeth's biographers.

The Reader-Engaged Classroom

Teachers with minority students have several concerns. One is how to meet their students' varied academic needs; related to that is the topic of fair testing. But underlying all of this is the question of student involvement. In what follows I am going to treat class work and student involvement together, as a joining of threads of "russet" and "honest kersey" that must take place before testing or extended independent written work is given. I am assuming a class where teacher and students interact orally.

The Play as Language

How do we get over the language hurdle in Shakespeare? Even Samuel Johnson complained that the reading of footnotes interrupts and chills the mind. This is true of our American-born students who have grown up speaking, writing, and thinking in English. With patience, and especially with an edition which presents footnotes to the side of the text rather than at the bottom, many of these students can and do learn to cope with footnotes. But bilingual students who are not yet fluent in English, or who perhaps have only recently learned to read and write in either their native language or in English, find the constant resort to footnotes frustrating. We might take a cue from George Bernard Shaw's for once generous praise of Shakespeare's "word music." The actress Melody Ryane, who has acted in both Shaw and Shakespeare at the Alabama Shakespeare Festival, says that Shakespeare is actually easier for actors to memorize and perform than Shaw, who wrote in prose, because of the rhythm in Shakespeare's prose and poetry.

This word music suggests a variety of strategies to the alert teacher. Teachers can try one or a combination of the following suggestions prior to assigning independent reading. Have the class listen to a taped version of a scene; class members themselves who are excellent student readers with a flair for the dramatic can be encouraged to do a taped reading of a scene. The teacher can do dramatic readings, especially of longer speeches. Arthea Reed, who has authored some teacher's guides to Shakespeare, recommends trying either choral reading, in which more than one person reads the same part at the same time, or story theatre, where one reads a part while another pantomimes the actions (1988, 11–12).

Choral reading or voicing is an untapped resource in the English classroom, perhaps because it seems old-fashioned. It has clear uses in Shakespeare, as for example in the witches' chants in *Macbeth*. Choral sounds can be tried, too. This spring Auburn University's theatre students did a *Midsummer Night's Dream* with fantastic fairies, making clicking sounds almost as continuous as the chorus of insects to be heard in the South. Dramaturge James Hammersmith's idea was to indicate through sound as well as costume and gesture that the fairies inhabited a special realm that was not the same as everyone else's five-senses reality. Teachers can try these sounds with their students: lovers' sighs, tears, and fears (Romeo, Juliet, Ophelia, Hamlet); malcontents' scoffings (Cassius, perhaps Hamlet and Macbeth); startled feet (Hamlet, Macbeth); and any other group chirping, growling, scowling that seems pertinent. In this context classes can try facial expressions as well.

Other prereading approaches are also available. Reed advises telling the story to the class (1988, 5). For teachers who are storytellers and natural hams, here's a chance to shine. The class can slow-act its way through a scene, with this acting interspersed with pointed, pithy teacher commentary and/or questions to the student actor. An example is, "How do you, Capulet, feel right now, when your nephew Tybalt is trying to start a brawl at your party?" Students can look at lines showing character traits and variations within one character, taken from throughout a play. These lines can include a mixture of styles, such as broken, halting speech, angry speech, poetically luxuriant speech, bombastic speech, foolish speech. The goal is to make students recognize variation in speakers, in fact to vary their "head" reading so that they hear a variety of voices in independent play reading. A list of sample lines to use is given in chapter 3.

Another approach is to ask students to hypothesize about situations before reading any Shakespeare text. The following suggestion for student consideration before reading *Julius Caesar* is offered by John Simmons:

> Suppose you had gone to school and grown up with a man, and he had grown very powerful and important while you had not. Then, as time went on and your jealousy increased, you began to feel more and more that he was getting drunk with power. What steps might you take towards him? (1968, 974–75)

Also, as a warm-up activity to prepare students for class acting once independent reading is assigned, the teacher can ask students to do narrative pantomimes. Show a character's encounter with a ghost or witch—show the expressions of both, show the power relationship, show the body language. (This exercise fits *Hamlet, Macbeth,* and *Julius Caesar.*) Show an encounter between a young person who is emotionally preoccupied and an older person who is somewhat sympathetic but basically lacking in understanding. (This exercise fits Polonius and the Nurse.) Try to talk someone into doing something. (This fits both Cassius's behavior and Mercutio's, as well as Lady Macbeth's.) Get festive and then get scolded (as do the idle mechanicals, i.e., workers, in *Julius Caesar*). Fall in love at first sight. Try to find out something (Romeo and Juliet asking the Nurse about each other's identity at the party; Polonius trying to learn the root of Hamlet's alteration). Think hard about a choice (Brutus, Hamlet, Macbeth), or make up your mind in an instant about what to do (Romeo). Read a document (the Capulet serving man, Hamlet, Brutus, Lady Macbeth).

Pantomime can also include such basic actions as eating, sleeping, nodding, and shaking the head "yes" or "no," which suit many stories or scenes. Teachers who have a packed curriculum with only a portion of the school year to devote to drama can be preparing ahead of time for drama by using pantomimes with stories and novels. This will serve at least two functions: (1) it will accustom the class members to thinking of the text as something realizable in human beings performing actions (think of Magwitch's deliciously described eating behavior, for example); (2) it will enable students to enter more fully into the world of the story or novel. For additional pantomime topics, see suggestions in Marjorie Vargas.

Once independent reading is assigned, the teacher can also assign students and doubles to individual roles or allow them to volunteer for those roles. Students will present their dramatic readings the next day in class. "A basic axiom to remember is that drama is most often a group art" (Heinig 1988, 62). Once students are drawn in by the story, the usual teacher role is diminished, or less apparently focal:

> It is generally assumed that the leader is the one responsible for implementing compensatory learning experiences. However, the classroom can also become a community of learners who willingly assist each other and help each other succeed. (61)

As students come to be more involved in the shaping of the actual class hour, the teacher does not abandon his or her responsibility. Mini-lessons on language points or points of social and political history relevant to the scenes being enacted can help clarify the meaning and function of certain lines. Because schools stress the strands of reading and writing in English curriculums more heavily than the strands of speaking, listening, and drama, students are more likely to ask questions about the kinds of topics I have focused on in this book: questions on the books and the speech of the time, plot construction and its context in social history, and the biography of the man Shakespeare.

The Play as Drama, the Students as Participants

Part of the great appeal and beauty of drama is the way it engages the emotions. Colonial and frontier Americans used performances of Shakespeare as entertainments for Native American peoples, including a 1752 performance of *Othello* before the Cherokee emperor and empress, who "sent their attendants to stop the killing on the stage" (Speaight 1973, 71). Drama stands lower, but not so far lower, than our own religious and moral instruction in its capacity to not only refine our affections but make us more imaginative and sympathetic persons. In fact, Shakespeare's drama had its roots in medieval church liturgy and medieval mystery plays. Additionally,

> Drama encourages participants to get *outside themselves.* Much of the stress we feel in our lives is the result of inward focus. (Heinig 1988, 63)

Many Shakespeareans have not only gotten lost in the plays themselves, but fancied themselves back in Shakespeare's England. Hodges imagined himself sitting in the Globe in the early morning air listening to a lecture by a German Shakespearean of the nineteenth century (1973, 96–97). Alfred Harbage imagined the complete texts of letters Shakespeare might have written to his wife, to his neighbor Hamnet Sadler, and to his kinsman Thomas Greene (1966, 139–44). Director Joseph Papp imagines Shakespeare staying up late to write Hamlet's famous "To be or not to be" soliloquy and having to stop to trim his quill. That accomplished, Papp's Shakespeare rushes out the next morning to read his work to Richard Burbage, still "snoring loudly, sprawled across his straw mattress," and who awakes to grumble " 'Dammit Will . . . can't you let an honest man sleep?' " (1988, viii).

Participation in classroom Shakespeare as actor or audience can be helped along by the Hodges pictures of the Globe Theatre (1973, 90–91) and of London in the time of Shakespeare (1949, inside back cover). By an exercise of the imagination, we too can bring Shakespeare alive again, taking him from his lodgings in Silver Street to the Blackfriars wharf, putting him into a little shoe-shaped boat, and sending him gliding across the Thames toward the Globe. When he disembarks, we can send him hurrying toward the storage lofts and dressing rooms to make sure all is well and in good order before the beginning of the 2:00 p.m. performance. Students who are not in the Lord Chamberlain's acting company (later the King's Men) can stand in the Globe yard, laughing, eating hazelnuts, drinking ale—rumbustious groundlings. Or, if they like, they can seat themselves in the galleries, wearing their elegant clothes and perfumed gloves, passing elegant compliments and elaborate jests, wishing to see and be seen.

Let's not forget Charney's emphasis on the accessibility of Shakespearean drama through the language of gesture and costume. Have students begin noticing in their daily lives the language of gesture and the situation in which their observations occur. Let them keep a journal. For example, even at so common a place as an ordinary ball field for a youth league baseball game, one notices and forgets almost more than can be written: the man who hitches his pants repeatedly; the man who scratches one leg with his other leg; the woman who keeps adjusting her glasses on her nose; the way uniformed children in the dugout imitate the umpire's definitive gesture for saying "Strike!"; or two babies, one running free and the other, wearing little appliquéd strawberries on a sunsuit, always watched over by a regardful parent. Then apply what can be applied to Shakespeare. Doesn't Hamlet imitate Osric? And the Nurse—she's always been watchful of Juliet, hasn't she? Or has she?

Teachers of high school freshmen can try to draw on whatever theatrical experiences their students have already had, no matter the level. For example, I recently accompanied a class of seventh graders to a stage production of *The Wizard of Oz.* The staging of the storm which transports Dorothy from Kansas to Oz was technically simple but highly effective, with its use of lighting, suggestive shadows, metallic ribbons, revolving props, and stylized gestures by those caught in the storm. Almost three centuries before the days of Edison, just how did the Jacobeans stage the storm scenes in King Lear? Perhaps just as they did *Julius Caesar,* referred to below. Sometimes we classroom teachers have to remind ourselves as much as our students that the use of staging materials in the Elizabethan theatre was spare, with language itself doing most of the creation and a receptive imagination supplying the rest.

Teachers who feel afraid or hesitant to try dramatics activities in the classroom because there would be no scenery can take comfort in the recollection of the unadorned nature of the Elizabethan stage. We, too, just like our students, are accustomed to modern realistic proscenium-arch conventions of staging. This, as much as a question about how the principal will react, is the cause of our fear.

The Wizard of Oz staging reinforced the sense in me that successful theatre depends on surprise, a point developed in chapter 6. Of course there is tension supplied in the story itself—by means of a plot complication as well as some means within the story for solving the dilemma—but there must always be an element of surprise, no matter how small, even in a very familiar story. This is why one of the following story summaries has greater dramatic potential than the other: "I came, I saw, I conquered" versus "I came, I partially saw, I struggled, and. . . ." Students can be brought to an explicit awareness through structured discussion. High school teachers of older students can draw on students' previous high school dramatics experiences and awarenesses.

Other backgrounds of experience students have had which secondary teachers can draw upon include participation in elementary school plays, May Days, ballet or other dance programs or recitals, church programs, and church pageants. Many churches at Christmastime have students dress up as Mary and Joseph, shepherds, angels, and wise men. Students enacting these roles might try to recall their feelings about acting the part of another person, using gestures to show emotion, and playing a role in front of an audience. Also, students can describe Halloween haunted houses. These contain visual elements, surprise, horror, and the grotesque—all prominent elements of Renaissance revenge plays.

Students can scan the story of a play just for the props it would take to stage it. For example, *Julius Caesar* requires thunder (drums or a rolled bullet in the Renaissance), lightning (fireworks or "blowing rosin through a candle flame"), and some form of scaffolding on stage for the body of Caesar during Antony's funeral speech, as well as firebrands on stage after Antony's speech (Charney, 1961, 44, 52, 60). One unexpected special effect needed for *Hamlet* is a fright wig (Charney 1969, 168). Someone might enjoy making a fright wig. Another is some form of picture of Hamlet Senior and Claudius. Miniatures in the Hilliard style are most probably what is intended. Students can be assigned to prop or costume committees.

Dramatic interpretations of individual key scenes can grow out of classroom discussions. For example, if one student sees the Nurse as genial, affectionate, and concerned, he can be deputized to assemble a cast for Act I, scene iii, projecting this premise. If another student states in discussion that the Nurse is meddlesome and annoying, she and a partner can do a reading of Act II, scene v, which projects this quality. In *How Tall Is This Ghost, John?* Australian teacher David Mallick offers a structured approach to deciding which of possible alternative readings should be given to a number of pivotal Shakespeare scenes.

Extension

Other possibilities for engaging minority students are noted in Heinig. Though her work focuses on a younger child, the ideas can be adapted to the needs and expressive capacities of the older child. For example, in asking students to tell stories from their culture, those to ask for in a Shakespearean context would be stories of love, political assassination, revenge, and ambition. Another idea is to ask students about entertainment and theatre traditions in their countries. The actor Richard Huggett has a funny chapter on the history of theatre disasters associated with performing *Macbeth,* including a disconcerting response of laughter from the audience at the sight of the beheaded Macbeth. Draw on students as much as possible for knowledge of their folk and literary culture. Ghostlore, for example, is relevant to the four Shakespeare tragedies studied in public school. Though critics normally look at such texts on witchcraft and the supernatural as Reginald Scot's or King James's, I find the account in Jesuit Father John Gerard's autobiography more compelling as testimony of what ordinary people really thought. The reader will recall from chapter 6 such episodes as that of the recently widowed Elizabethan countryside woman who felt a spectral disturbance in her bedroom for a month after her husband's death (1951, 179).

Multiple, festive responses to Shakespeare are possible and almost sure to appeal to everyone including the principal—if things are well organized. Students can work toward a medieval/Renaissance fair, taking cues from the literary text about the directions in which to develop.

Romeo and Juliet includes music, banqueting, and sword fighting, as well as herb lore; *Hamlet* and *Macbeth* are both set in a castle; *Hamlet* also includes music and a theatrical entertainment as well. Harbage has gathered together Shakespeare's lyrics and some musical scores in *Shakespeare's Songs;* they can be played on a portable electronic keyboard. Alternately, recordings of Renaissance consort and madrigal music are available. Medieval and Renaissance recipes are available in the wonderful book *Fabulous Feasts* by Madeleine Pelner Cosman. I have made the saumon pie (1976, 172) and parsley bread (156–57), and have drunk the blushing ypocras (spiced red wine, 154) with a sallat (medieval salad, 185). A description of medieval and Renaissance games is available in the article by Roger Pringle, "Sports and Recreations." James A. Warner and Margaret J. White have written a book about Shakespeare's flowers; herb lore is found in many books. For possibilities, explore health food stores or nurseries as well as bookstores. Excellent paper models of medieval castles are available.[1] Teachers interested in developing games involving historical knowledge can do so using facts from their history textbooks or literature anthologies and following a "Wheel of Fortune" or "Jeopardy" format.

The 1985 National Teacher of the Year, Terry Dozier, offered her lesson plan for a medieval fair which culminated a six-week unit of work. Student activities on which research was done included a puppet show, merelles,[2] archery, trumpeters, chess, quoits (a game like ringtoss), backgammon, arm wrestling, staff combat, minstrels, trapball, and a human chess match. The order of the fair was: grand procession, medieval play, medieval music and dancing, browsing through guild tents and viewing demonstrations and competitions, mental jousting,[3] athletic competitions, human chess match, great feast. Themes of the fair included medieval personalities, warfare, life-styles, art and architecture, the plague, the Crusades, recreation, issues of the church, myths, legends, and wizardry (1985, 103).

Details of social history can make small but serendipitous contributions to our understanding of Shakespeare. One example comes from festivals and food. The setting of *Romeo and Juliet*, for example, is in mid-July, hot days when the "mad blood" stirs. Beneath this calendar time, a dangerous time for humor-engendered passions, runs a contrapuntal note from the liturgical calendar. Lady Capulet says it is "a fortnight and odd days" to Lammastide, and the Nurse says Juliet's birthday is "Lammas Eve at night." Lammas was a high summer church festival; "it was marked by a church celebration blessing grains and breads, and offering thanks to God for a good harvest." The festival itself was celebrated with breads—some fruit breads, some colored saffron or rose or green, some shaped in amusing ways. One festival bread was rose-petal bread (see figure 1). The accompanying drink might have been lamb's wool, "the splendid warm spiced cider with frothy baked apples floating on top" (see figure 2) (Cosman 1981, 73, 75).

These foods can still be made today. I have made them as part of a workshop on Shakespeare for teachers. In a modern kind of interlude (see the description of Judith Rosenfeld's interlude in note 4), at the halfway point in our text-oriented discussion on a warm August

Rose-Petal Bread

2 packages active dry yeast
2 cups warm water
6 tablespoons honey
7 cups unbleached white or whole wheat flour
1 ⅔ tablespoons coarse salt
6 whole eggs plus 1 egg yolk
1 cup currants, softened in warm water
6 tablespoons melted butter or oil

butter for greasing bowls and cookie sheet
1½ teaspoons dried rosemary
1½ teaspoons dried basil
½ teaspoon cinnamon
⅔ or 1 cup finely chopped rose petals (between 1 and 2 doz. red roses)*
several drops red food paint, prepared as the medieval baker would, in advance**

1. Sprinkle the yeast on ½ cup of the warm water in a mixing bowl. Stir in the honey. Let it stand for 5 minutes.
2. Add the remaining warm water and about 2½ to 3 cups of flour. Beat by hand with a wooden spoon, about 200 strokes. Cover with a damp towel, put in a warm place, and let the dough rise 30 to 45 minutes, or until it is doubled in bulk.
3. Punch the dough down. Beat in the salt, melted butter, and 5 whole eggs plus 1 egg yolk. Stir in the currants.
4. In a mortar with a pestle, crush the rosemary, basil, cinnamon, and rose petals to make a paste. Add this herb mixture to the dough and knead it, blending well. (The bread should be a delicate rose hue. If the color from the rose petals isn't strong enough, use the red food color sparingly).
5. Beat in the remaining flour, using a spoon. Knead the dough until it comes away from the sides of the bowl.
6. Turn the dough out onto a lightly floured board or slab of marble and knead it until smooth, shiny, or elastic, about 10–12 minutes, adding small amounts of flour if the dough becomes too sticky to handle.
7. Place the dough in a buttered bowl. Cover with a damp towel. Let it rise in a warm place until doubled in bulk, about 50 minutes.
8. Punch the dough down. Cover it, and let it rise again until doubled in bulk, about 30 minutes.
9. Again, punch the dough down. Turn it out onto a floured surface and let it rest for 5 minutes. Shape the dough into 1 or 2 free-form, turbanlike curls or twists. Place on a buttered cookie sheet. Cover lightly with a towel and let it rise in a warm place until doubled in bulk, about 25 minutes.
10. Preheat the oven to 375°. Brush the loaf or loaves with the remaining whole egg, lightly beaten. Bake for about 50 minutes or until nicely browned and the loaf sounds hollow when rapped lightly on the top with knuckles. Transfer the rose-petal bread to a rack and allow it to cool.

* It is advisable to obtain roses, either from a florist or a garden, that have not been sprayed with pesticides.

** Remember that the chief cook was considered a food artist. In addition to natural colors of fruits, vegetables, creams, and meats, the cook would add natural "food paint" or color to invigorate paler or duller hues, or to create special illusions. Today's natural vegetable dyes are simply the modern versions of medieval food paints, which were created by boiling flowers or leaves in water or white wine. For medieval red food coloring, rose petals were used; for yellow and gold, saffron or dandelion; for green, mint, parsley, spinach, or hazel leaves; for blue, heliotrope or turnsole; for lavender, violets.

Figure 1. Recipe for rose-petal bread. (Source: Cosman 1976, 116, 119–20.)

Lamb's Wool

This gently spiced cider can be made in a variety of ways, so long as the drink has "lamb's wooly" apples and cream floating on its surface. Some medieval recipes suggest baking apples till they burst; others recommend roasting, broiling, or boiling. The apple cider suggested here is not alcoholic; however, some recipes substitute for the cider a dry white wine, a light ale, or stout beer. Depending upon the season for its serving, *lamb's wool* may be drunk warm or cool.

1 gallon apple cider

½ cup sugar, to be added if apple cider is very tart

⅛ teaspoon ground nutmeg

¼ teaspoon powdered cinnamon

½ teaspoon powdered ginger

12 small apples, peeled with cores removed

2 cups heavy whipping cream

¼ teaspoon salt

2 tablespoons brown sugar

1. In a large enameled pot, slowly heat ¾ of the cider, until warm but not boiling.
2. In another enameled pot pour remaining cider, and add the apples, sugar, nutmeg, cinnamon, and ginger, and bring to a boil. Vigorously simmer the apples until they lose their shape and become "frothy."
3. Pour ¾ of the cider into a large glass serving bowl, which has been slightly heated so that the warm fluid will not crack it.
4. Pour the remaining hot cider with the spiced apples into the serving bowl.
5. Whip the cream with the salt and brown sugar until it peaks.
6. Spoon the cream onto the lamb's wool, or add the cream to each tankard of lamb's wool as it is served.

Figure 2. Recipe for lamb's wool. (Source: Cosman 1976, 131.)

morning, we stopped for bread and beverage. We listened to Renaissance music, including Shakespearean songs from the Deller Consort on an RCA recording. Other available recordings include Nonesuch's *In a Medieval Garden*, the RCA Deller recording of *O Ravishing Delight*, and Nonesuch's *Renaissance Choral Music for Christmas*. We also looked at the book, *Shakespeare's Flowers* (Warner and White 1987), which shows the kinds of roses Shakespeare had seen in England before he ever wrote Juliet's line about roses and names. *Shakespeare's Birds* (Goodfellow 1983) shows the birds Shakespeare had seen in England, birds mentioned in Romeo and Juliet's aubade. One of my workshop participants planned to take a slice of rose-petal bread to his girlfriend. Every one of us thought of this as a sweet and romantic gesture.

Somehow, the bread, music, and books helped us to recognize the intense but brief feeling of love and happiness felt by Romeo and

Juliet. A Lammas game described by Cosman (1981, 75) in which couples compete for the honor of being declared the most harmonious underscores the link between the fruitfulness of the earth and the fruitfulness of love. Also, the Lammas custom of saving a quarter loaf for a year, finally to be fed to the birds, underscores the full cycle of birth, death, and regeneration in human life.

The recipes which follow are taken from Cosman's *Medieval Holidays and Festivals.* In my baking experience, a small damask rose, which herbalists call the old country rose or old garden rose, will work well in this recipe. (The reader is cautioned that a cup of petals from a florist's variety of roses will make this a very expensive bread. Find a rose donor in the neighborhood or out in the country instead.) The flowers should not be sprayed with insecticides, and the reader should resist the temptation to wash the roses. As a French woman who works in a local health food store explained to me, that would take away the delicate rose flavor. Instead, the reader may prepare the petals by gently wiping each petal. This recipe braids very attractively and easily. I do not use food colorings, finding enough color and excitement yielded from the sight of the petals against the tawny-colored bread. But a bit of red dye can be used to make the bread slightly pink. I once made parsley bread for trenchers for a medieval feast. The amount of parsley was more than enough to give the bread a greenish—but interesting—cast. The lamb's wool is very good cool or warm. Bon Appetit!

Written Assignments and Testing

Maryland middle school teacher Judith B. Rosenfeld has offered excellent ideas for introducing Shakespeare to middle school children. Her culmination in "An Elizabethan Interlude" resembles Terry Dozier's fair, but at a seventh- or eighth-grade level. The writing assignments before the interlude[4] are especially helpful. Sonnet summaries took the form of "telegrams of ten words or less on yellow kraft paper [written] with black felt pens" (1987, 50). One sample was: "Dissatisfied with myself, thinking of you fills me with Delight!" for Sonnet 24 ("When in disgrace with fortune and men's eyes"). Winter poetry was inspired by the "Winter's Poem" from *Love's Labour's Lost* and decorated with borders resembling those in Barbara Holdridge's collection of Shakespeare's poetry for children. Under the spell of *Romeo and Juliet,* students used Shakespearean lyrics to make "valentines out of glitter, doilies, and colorful pens and markers" (1987, 50). During their study, Rosenfeld's students viewed a film on castles based on Macaulay's book. They also viewed the Glenda Jackson movie, *Elizabeth, the Cub.* At the interlude itself, students wore masks they had created; presented information *in persona* about Elizabethan medicine, education, science, etc.; did dramatic readings; played music and did a group dance.

Older students would enjoy aspects of these activities but are also ready for research topics. Some under-researched and therefore controllable topics relate to Shakespeare's female characters as well as to the women who have actually acted in Shakespearean drama. Steven Lynn explains feminism simply as "reading as a woman would" (1990, 268). Students with an interest in feminism might want to explore the life and career of the nineteenth-century American actress Charlotte Cushman, who played Romeo to her sister's Juliet, as well as Hamlet, Cardinal Wolsey, and a number of female roles. Students might also be interested in looking into what was evidently a nineteenth-century rage for female Hamlets (see Winter [1911] 1969, 237–442). This topic can potentially generate fruitful discussion and/or performance. Other interesting female Shakespeareans were the eighteenth-century Sarah Siddons, said to have been the best Lady Macbeth ever, and the late nineteenth-/early twentieth-century actress Ellen Terry. African American students might enjoy reading about such historical actors as Ira Aldridge. In addition, there are many African American actors playing Shakespearean roles now, including Kent Gash as *Twelfth Night*'s Feste and Derrick Weeden as *Macbeth*'s Malcolm in the 1989–1990 Alabama Shakespeare Festival Repertoire. Also of interest is the way Shakespeare has been received in countries other than English-speaking countries. Anne Paolucci's article is a good starting point.

In chapter 2 I use Steven Lynn's explanation of reader-response criticism as building a reading from the reader's subjective responses. This approach can be extremely productive in the classroom. On pages 25–26 I present seven topics as writing assignments. The teacher who wishes to use any of these can modify them in the ways suggested there. Teachers using the second topic might also ask students to critique their own performances and staging choices. After the writing topics, I list questions that encourage students who are reluctant to see drama as presentational to develop a sense of the dramatic in their own lives.

Now we turn to the issue of testing. A fair test will follow up on language, scenes, points, and themes highlighted in class. One of my most successful testing experiences came from an 80 percent minority class studying *Julius Caesar*. Besides viewing a movie of the play, we also read the play, viewed a silent filmstrip which summarized the action and quoted famous quotes, and worked together in an interactive format with me at the overhead projector developing notes on the play.

If this sounds like saturated Shakespeare, it is more palatable for all involved than the "Shakespeare Lite" served up in prewrapped slices of publisher fill-in-the-blank ersatz drama.

If all of this involvement produces no better than a *Tom Jones*'s Partridge at the theatre, with the eighteenth-century provincialism of his reference to "Squire Hamlet" and his criticism of the nonworking gravedigger, we have nonetheless succeeded in developing learners excited about a new contemporary, Señor Shakespeare. However, I think this approach will produce much better than Partridge. Moreover, the activities suggested will engage the whole class, not just this or that portion of the class.

An Epilogue for the Teacher

Many things can help in implementing a reader-response classroom. (1) Be aware of what is popular now. Watch some MTV for video conventions and watch a few situation comedies for plotting conventions and stock characters. Be aware of the Nielsen ratings and their implications. For instance, it has recently been said that people are watching television at work. In Elizabethan England, just at the dawn of modern capitalism, workers had little incentive to work beyond subsistence, as is amply testified to by the sermons of the day against idleness and drink (Hirst 1986, 3). Perhaps this built-in leisure was one factor contributing to the availability of a London audience for Shakespeare's plays. Apprentices were among Shakespeare's Globe audience (see Gurr 1987). (2) Read Lawrence Levine on Shakespeare in America in the nineteenth century. His plays were vastly popular, readily intermingled with minstrel shows. Now that he's become high culture, some of that accessibility is gone. (3) Adopt ideas from books oriented to younger children, such as *100+ Ideas for Drama* (Scher and Verrall 1975). In a packed curriculum, a teacher can work in with short story reading earlier in the school year such exercises in dramatic techniques as concentration, projection, method, voice modulation, and eye contact. (4) Be eclectic in other ways, too. Foreign language teachers have some wonderful ideas for classroom playlets which involve everybody in plots structured by incremental repetition. (5) Recognize the specific talents of those gifted in music (this can be used for Renaissance music) or athletics (for duels). Don't stereotype. Some people are multitalented. (6) Save things which can make good props: hats, masks, mirrors, handbags. Also, note the basic plots given in *100+ Ideas for Drama* (81–99). (7) If you are not satisfied with filmstrips available on Shakespeare's historical period, construct your own slide show and commentary by using the illustrations available in books on Shakespeare's life and times.

We can structure our lives by all kinds of means—stories, metaphors, catchy mottoes, or analyses. Barbara Christian criticizes literary criticism's recent deformation, suggesting criticism only became prominent at all as certain critics adopted the view that the Western literary tradition suffered a decline in the twentieth century and was threatened with being replaced by the writing of African American and Caribbean and other Third World writers (1988, 71). Some recent academic criticism does indeed make bizarre reading. Drama, with its use of presented story as a way of engaging the audience's mind, spirit, and imagination, is much closer to the purpose and heart of living than are these dry intellectual studies. We are all the happier for it.

Moreover, our classes will perform better if they are engaged by a text. They may even perform better on the writing test portion of the National Assessment of Educational Progress achievement tests if their own work in their literature classroom has stimulated them to take a keener interest in their own writing.[5] They will enjoy and remember their work more. Let's not be afraid to try something different in class just for fear of the office, the parents, or colleagues. Our students as once and future citizens are our primary clients.

————————

Teacher checkpoint. In this chapter we stayed in our classrooms, imagining them "stately furnished scenes" and seeing them as no more unworthy scaffolds than the buskin-trodden boards of the busy Elizabethan stage. We reviewed many approaches for involving students as actors, readers, and interpreters of Shakespeare.

Notes

1. Such castles are available from Usborne Publishing Ltd., 20 Garrick Street, London WC2E 9BJ, England. Readers can also write to the Canadian publisher, which is Hayes Publishing Ltd., 3312 Mainway, Burlington, Ontario, Canada L7M 1A7, and should specify Usborne Cut-Out Models, "Cut-Out Model Castle." Readers can also consult the Caldecott Honor Book by David Macaulay, *Castle,* Boston: Houghton Mifflin, 1977.

2. "Merelles" is a French-derived word with various English spellings, which refers either to the game pieces or more properly to the board game itself, a game the English refer to as "nine men's morris." Sid Sackson has collected a set of board games which includes nine men's morris. The book of rules, which includes game boards and pieces, is entitled *The Book of Classic*

Board Games. The publisher is Klutz Press, 2121 Staunton Court, Palo Alto, CA 94306. The copyright is 1991.

3. In this game students studying world history researched answers to questions having to do with the Middle Ages and themes of the fair. Each class chose representatives who "jousted" for the honor of being "supreme medieval scholar" (Dozier 1985).

4. An "evening of sharing" in which students wore self-designed masks embodying Elizabethan roles they represented, did dramatic readings, sang, danced, and sampled Elizabethan recipes (Rosenfeld 1987, 51).

5. Frances C. Fowler analyzes why comparative education specialists ranked France *first* "in the teaching of the native tongue" and the United States *last*. She concludes that "The total education environment in which French teachers work supports the teaching of writing. The total educational environment in the United States does not" (1989, 71).

8 Conclusion

This book on Shakespeare's social and political surroundings was written for schoolteachers. Stanley Wells, the general editor of the Oxford Shakespeare, recognizes his own work as part of the coral reef of textual editorial work (1984, 3). Writing for practicing classroom teachers is another coral reef, though one not yet as deep and treacherous as the Great Barrier Reef off Australia or the textual reef off the 1623 Folio.

I first learned of Shakespeare's mixture of the homely and the magical from such lyrics studied in high school as "Tu-who, Tu-whit, tu-who: a merry note, / While greasy Joan doth keel the pot." I, too, had an Aunt Joan and was intrigued. From the clear, single recorder notes of this lyric, my mind went on to an almost rhapsodic view of the tragedies, each an exquisite, flawless, richly colored jewel of language, enveloped in the magnificently gloomy jewelry box of heavy velvets and intricate brocades, somber lighting, and stark, dark-stained sets. The comedies were something lighter, less musky and Port wine-like, perhaps a pieced and knotted garden, blown over by a fragrant breeze.

I see the plays less imagistically now. A parent-chaperone who attended *Romeo and Juliet* with my classes remarked after the play, "It makes you feel as though you've been through it yourself." Like this woman, I feel this twisting and turning more now. I also see Shakespeare as upholding an ethic of life, a valuable message in a time which often seems to uphold only the marketplace.

I also see Shakespeare's historical time as inexhaustibly rich and varied, with material to hand from many corners—history; biography; studies of medieval and Elizabethan theatre, including stage construction and stage conventions, audience composition, and acting companies—which yield insights.

The greater factuality of such materials seems enhanced to me in middle age, and the glow which once surrounded works of literary criticism seems distinctly less ethereal and more gaseous to me now than it did when I was a newly graduated, proud possessor of a B.A. in philosophy over two decades ago. The New Critics, those once lofty Olympians, seem exposed and betrayed by their successors, the deconstructionists. Both tribes take a woven garment and unravel it, using the yarn to rework a story, placing together what images or ideas they please, regardless of the location in the originally told story.

Readers of history can be guilty of myth, too. Those interested in the historical approach should beware of falling into a myth trap: fairy-tale England, where the imprisoned Mary, Queen of Scots, comes to seem like a bewitched damsel in a tale, rather than the courageous woman she was at the end of her life; or gallant England of the fancy court, with the pearled and bewigged Queen of the "Ditchley" portrait, standing in white satin shoes on Ditchley, Oxfordshire, on a map of Europe, the courtier Walter Raleigh writing languid poetry, captaining dashing sea adventures, and chivalrously spreading his cloak over water for the Queen. These myths ignore Elizabeth's penury, shown in her willingness to take Lord Burghley's advice about saving money on the salaries of the Armada survivors (Martin and Parker 1988, 253, 259); or Raleigh's languishing in the Tower from 1603 until his execution in 1618, with one reprieve to go on his ill-fated mission to the Orinoco in search of gold; or merry, lusty England, full of quips, puns, beer, green countryside, sheep, morris dancers, and apple-cheeked serving maids selling oranges and more at the theatres. Finally, there is the myth of quaint England. Those seeing Sir Henry Peacham's sketch of the stage performance of *Titus Andronicus* (Smith 1967, 298–99) might be tempted to think, "What charming little Elizabethans." Those little Elizabethans lived in an age of religious bloodshed, bombast, and brilliance abounding, not an age of tea in flowered bone china cups in damasked and draped Victorian drawing rooms.

But the historians themselves are pretty good about avoiding myths these days. They present a different picture of the Elizabethan and Jacobean periods than some Shakespearean literary critics have. While the latter write in warm, glowing tones about the herbs, tooth-paste, gardens, and home remedies, blowing a warm, perfumed sweetness over the reader's pictured scene, the historians present a rather grim view, one of appalling hygiene, lack of medicines, a population stopped from modern standards of productivity by a griping in the gut or a toothache, a dunghill or wandering pig as obstacle in a market town, blowing thereby a different odor over the reader's pictured scene.

I find comfort in the fact that our own age is not so aberrant when I locate analogous situations in the past:

- For those who say our college students only value money, power, and image, note that Machiavelli's book was a best seller in its time, going through twenty-five editions from 1532–1552.

- The Stuarts used thin forces to pull up "illegal tobacco crops in the west country" (a crop introduced by gallant Walter Raleigh, incidentally) to little avail (Morrill 1984, 299); likewise our attempt at alcohol prohibition after World War I with the passage of the Eighteenth Amendment proved futile, as evidenced by the passage of the Twenty-first Amendment, which repealed Prohibition in 1933.

- The sixfold increase in the size of the staff servicing the courts of law and the Privy Council during the reigns of James I and Charles I "did not improve on Elizabethan levels of efficiency" (301); likewise the burgeoning White House administrative staff is only one example of an expansion in administrative positions which does not guarantee increased efficiency.

- "Englishmen were notoriously litigious" (304), pressing 20,000 suits a year, with the average Chancery battle lasting twenty-three years (Baker 1985, 42); Shakespeare himself went to court for petty sums of money. Half of the cases heard in ecclesiastical courts were sexual sins.

- The scandalous trials of Frances Howard, first for divorce from the Earl of Essex (son of Elizabeth's onetime favorite) on the grounds of his impotence and later Frances's murder trial for poisoning Sir Thomas Overbury were both titillating in their time, the latter trial "eagerly followed in 1613 by manuscript newsletters in country houses across England" (Hirst 1986, 116). I doubt that any location in the country is short of sensationalized trials. Possible recent parallels include the amount of attention given the Senate hearings to confirm Clarence Thomas to the Supreme Court, with the riveting point/counterpoint testimony of Clarence Thomas and Anita Hill, or the William Kennedy Smith rape trial.

Besides these perspectives and correctives from history, what else of use to a teacher can be learned from an inquiry into the Renaissance? Many things. The Renaissance Elizabethan theatre was grounded in medieval theatre traditions and had definite links with liturgical practice and biblical beliefs. The universality of Shakespeare's plays comes partly as a result of his skirting the censor of the day. Moreover, not only the existence of an office of Master of Revels, but the Act of Uniformity enforcing belief in the Church of England and the Sumptuary Laws regulating the colors and materials individuals could wear, all indicate that Shakespeare's society was much more controlled than ours.

Society then was more communal, from boat travel on the Thames, to the love of group singing, to the availability of instruments for use in barbershops or taverns. This contrasts sharply with our cultural emphasis on privacy and individualism, noted in such things as cars with only one occupant (the driver), the use of music headphones, and magazines set out for reading in doctors' and hairdressers' waiting areas. In that society with no newspapers or televisions, a smaller number of events were given more prominence, from the sailing of the Armada, to the capturing of individual Jesuits, to the death of Elizabeth and coronation of James, to the Overbury murder and trial. In fact, it seems that the difficulty of travel and the lack of a variety of technologically enabled entertainments were subtle factors contributing to the popularity of drama.

A different view of intertextuality obtained in Shakespeare's time. He could use sources without footnoting originators. Now we must credit every view, discovery, or error by name and date. Shakespeare was lucky in his friends, John Heminge and Henry Condell. Now our public figures don't trust to luck or friends, but, like Nancy Reagan, must have "their turn" in print. To think of Shakespeare as researching his plays in a modern scholarly manner is to ignore such matters as when the printing press was invented (and, hence, how available books were), when such tools as encyclopedias and dictionaries were invented, and the facts that Shakespeare was not university educated, that historical accuracy was not of utmost importance to the acting company for which Shakespeare wrote (for eyewitness testimony, see Henry Peacham's sketch of *Titus Andronicus* [reproduced in Smith 1967, 298–99], a Roman play in the makeshift "Roman" dress available to the company), that the acting repertory system was extremely demanding for the performers (see Beckerman 1962, 23 for details), and that theatres were creating illusions, not scholarly accuracy.

Elizabethan England did not section off drama from life as much as we do today. Capital punishments were capital entertainment; animal entrails were used for added realism and shock value in execution scenes in plays; and the age was far more preoccupied with religious doctrines, practices, and disputes than Western society is today.

There was a love of display, grandeur, rhetoric, and allegory. To appreciate this, one need only consider the elaborate entertainments for Queen Elizabeth at Elvetham in Hampshire given by the Earl of Hertford, or James I's triumphal arches (Hodges 1973, 70–71), or the theatrical allegory of rumor as a character wearing painted tongues. "Subtleties" in cooking—little disguised surprises such as birds baked in a pie—were matched or outdone by "subtleties" in inlaid furniture, herb gardens, ornate book printing, clothing, and rhetoric. Slash a sleeve on a doublet and underclothing of contrasting color and texture might be revealed, as in the lordly portraits of Henry VIII by Holbein. It should not be surprising, then, that Shakespeare's plays are rhetorically luxuriant. The use of metaphor and simile seemed common in prose as well as in poetry. Metaphor was in their eyes then; see, for example, the picture in Nicoll (no. 417) entitled "Draught of a Ship compared with a Fish" (a larger reproduction can be found in Smith 1967, 340–41). This varied exuberance contrasts rather startlingly with twentieth-century outlooks. Our current vogue for cookbooks, for instance, seems to come from a desire for a guaranteed correct and uniform result as well as from a breakdown of oral routes of knowledge transmission.

Many factors were necessary to the Elizabethan theatre we know. A number of the factors are concomitants of the invention of the printing press and the presence of books in society. The voyages of discovery and the ascendancy of London; the Latin curriculum of the English grammar school, with its emphasis on classics, poetry, and rhetoric; the literacy of players and playwrights; the classical learning of translators and their interest in the vernacular; the Reformation itself and Elizabeth's tolerance of humanistic expression are all related at least in part to the presence of print in the sixteenth century. Aspects of story plotting can be variously traced to the physical dimensions and design of the theatres, contemporaneous events, and medieval theatre traditions. Much of this is discussed in my chapters on books and on plotting.

Retired Shakespearean Norman Brittin has said of the work being done on Shakespeare: "There is something helpful in every corner." My advice to teachers is to read widely by taste and inclination. Good teachers realize that more information will be absorbed by the teacher from the printed page than can be presented in a class lecture. But good teachers always have something extra in reserve.

Another point is to realize where the appeal of a particular play will lie for a particular class. *Romeo and Juliet* combines themes of youth versus age, individual love versus family feud, humanity versus the universe, and also a certain isolation of the protagonists. The play meets with responsiveness from our students because they also experience isolation: as children in day care, as latchkey children, and as passive victims of technological isolation wrought by Walkmans, television, cars, Nintendos, etc. Unfortunately, part of the isolation seems also to come from moral, intellectual, and spiritual drifting in some quarters of society, which results in a feeling of emptiness or hollowness.

As long as we are able to project ourselves into the views of others, we have both learned something and expanded our moral sensitivity. Our emerging nations and minorities offer us the possibility of recognizing a great writer whose reputation will rival Shakespeare's. This writer will not come from the overeducated, court-refined kind of minority, however; he or she will be someone of the people. This writer will come from a society with a popular tradition, someone who has a respect for many kinds of people and a love of their language, someone with faith in God, maybe Lord of the purple fields and not just of the white sideboard church, someone with a smattering (Elizabethan style) of a "classical" language training (not necessarily in Latin), someone from a building nation, in ascendancy, with great expectations.

The great Shakespeare library, the Folger, has stained-glass windows on one wall of the reading room depicting the journey of the individual through the seven ages of man. I suppose many of us teachers are in the fifth stage, personified as the justice:

> In fair round belly with good capon lined,
> with eyes severe and beard of formal cut,
> full of wise saws and modern instances.
> (As You Like It, II.vii.154–56)

But, like cholesterol-conscious moderns, we eschew the capon for the grilled, skinless breast of chicken, many of us beardless as women not witches, with softened mien and few maxims. Given this radically modified picture of the justice, I am seeking to forge links with that remarkably unaltered other,

> . . . the whining schoolboy, with his satchel
> and shining morning face, creeping like snail
> Unwillingly to school.
> (145–47)

Only now we should add, we give equal attention to schoolgirls, too. For the sake of all shining morning faces, this book has been written. We teachers revel in the puddle jumpers.[1] They make us young again, alive again, in the true tradition of Shakespearean romance.

Note

1. A sculpture on the grounds of the Alabama Shakespeare Festival in Montgomery depicts a group of boys and girls running, laughing, skipping, and holding hands. It is entitled "Puddle Jumpers."

Works Cited

Allen, Diane. 1990. "NCTE to You." *English Journal* 70.2: 90–91.

Anderson, Robert, et al., eds. 1989. *Elements of Literature: Third Course.* Austin: Holt, Rinehart and Winston.

Andrews, John F., ed. 1985. *William Shakespeare: His World, His Work, His Influence.* 3 volumes. New York: Scribner's Sons.

Baker, J. H. "Law and Legal Institutions." In Andrews, 1985, 41–54.

Barber, Charles. 1982. "The English Language in the Age of Shakespeare." In *The New Pelican Guide to English Literature: The Age of Shakespeare,* vol. 2, pt. 2, edited by Boris Ford, 227–44. New York: Penguin.

Barroll, Leeds. 1988. "A New History for Shakespeare and His Time." *Shakespeare Quarterly* 39: 441–64.

Baugh, Albert C., and Thomas Cable. 1978. *A History of the English Language.* 3rd ed. Englewood Cliffs, NJ: Prentice-Hall.

Beckerman, Bernard. 1962. *Shakespeare at the Globe, 1599–1609.* New York: Macmillan.

Beerbohm, Max. 1977. *Beerbohm's Literary Caricatures: From Homer to Huxley.* Edited by J. G. Riewald. Hamden, CT: Archon.

Berry, Ralph. 1988. *Shakespeare and Social Class.* Atlantic Highlands, NJ: Humanities.

Betken, William T., ed. 1984. *The Other Shakespeare: "Romeo and Juliet."* Rhinebeck, NY: Bardavon Books.

Bevington, David, ed. 1988. *Macbeth,* by William Shakespeare. New York: Bantam.

Bishop, Morris. 1970. *The Middle Ages.* New York: American Heritage Press.

Brinkworth, E.R.C. 1972. *Shakespeare and the Bawdy Court of Stratford.* Chichester: Phillimore.

Bullough, Geoffrey. 1973. *Narrative and Dramatic Sources of Shakespeare.* Vol. 7. New York: Columbia University Press.

Burgess, Anthony. 1970. *Shakespeare.* New York: Knopf.

Byrne, Muriel St. Clare. "Elizabethan Life in the Plays." In Campbell and Quinn, 1966, 202–07.

———, ed. 1981. *Lisle Letters: An Abridgement.* Selected and arranged by Bridget Boland. Chicago: University of Chicago Press.

Campbell, Oscar James, and Edward G. Quinn, eds. 1966. *The Reader's Encyclopedia of Shakespeare.* New York: Crowell.

Carter, Avis Murton. 1973. *One Day in Shakespeare's England.* New York: Abelard-Schuman.

Charney, Maurice. 1961. *Shakespeare's Roman Plays.* Cambridge: Harvard University Press.

————. *Style in "Hamlet."* 1969. Princeton: Princeton University Press.

————. "Contemporary Issues in Shakespearean Interpretation." In Andrews, 1985, 889–911.

Christian, Barbara. 1988. "The Race for Theory." *Feminist Studies* 14: 67–79.

Cole, Douglas, comp. 1970. *Twentieth Century Interpretations of "Romeo and Juliet."* Englewood Cliffs, NJ: Prentice-Hall.

Coleman, D. C. "Economic Life in Shakespeare's England." In Andrews, 1985, 67–73.

Colman, E.A.M. 1974. *The Dramatic Use of Bawdy in Shakespeare.* London: Longmans.

Cosman, Madeleine Pelner. 1976. *Fabulous Feasts: Medieval Cookery and Ceremony.* New York: Braziller.

————. 1981. *Medieval Holidays and Festivals.* New York: Scribner's Sons.

Creighton, Mandel. 1893. *The Age of Elizabeth.* New York: Scribner's Sons.

Crowley, Sharon. 1989. *A Teacher's Introduction to Deconstruction.* Urbana: NCTE.

Day, Richard. 1578. *A Booke of Christian Prayers.* London.

Dent, R. W. 1981. *Shakespeare's Proverbial Language.* Berkeley: University of California Press.

Dollimore, Jonathan, and Alan Sinfield. 1985. *Political Shakespeare.* Ithaca: Cornell University Press.

Dozier, Terry. 1985. "World History Lesson Plan." *Today's Education:* 103.

Dwyer, Frank. 1988. *Henry VIII.* New York: Chelsea.

Edwards, Francis, S.J. 1985. *The Jesuits in England.* Tunbridge Wells: Burns and Oates.

Eisenstein, Elizabeth L. 1979. *The Printing Press as an Agent of Change.* Vol. 1. Cambridge, England: Cambridge University Press.

Erickson, Carolly. 1983. *The First Elizabeth.* New York: Summit.

Evans, G. Blakemore, ed. 1984. *Romeo and Juliet.* The New Cambridge Shakespeare. Cambridge, England: Cambridge University Press.

Evans, Maurice. 1951. "Elizabethan Spoken English." *Cambridge Journal* 4: 401–14.

Farnham, Willard, ed. *Hamlet.* In Harbage, 1969, 930–76.

Fella, Thomas. 1585–1622. *A Booke of Diveirs Devises.* Commonplace book. Washington: The Folger Shakespeare Library.

Filteau, Jerry. 1990. "Moyers: TV Has Power to Shape Human Values." *The Catholic Week* 55.69 (April 27): 5.

Foster, Donald W. 1987. "Master W. H., R.I.P." *PMLA* 102: 42–54.

Fowler, Frances. 1989. "Why François Knows How to Write." *English Journal* 78.2: 71–74.

Fox, Levi. 1972. *Shakespeare's England.* New York: Putnam.

Fraser, Antonia. 1969. *Mary Queen of Scots.* New York: Dell.

————. 1975a. *King James VI of Scotland, I of England.* New York: Knopf.

————, ed. 1975b. *The Lives of the Kings and Queens of England.* New York: Knopf.

————. 1984. *The Weaker Vessel.* New York: Knopf.

Frey, Charles. 1984. "Teaching Shakespeare in America." *Shakespeare Quarterly* 35: 541–59.

Frye, Roland Mushat. 1967. *Shakespeare's Life and Times.* Princeton: Princeton University Press.

————. 1984. *The Renaissance "Hamlet."* Princeton: Princeton University Press.

Gallo, Donald R. 1988. "Joseph Papp: The Man Who Brings Shakespeare to Life." *English Journal* 77.7: 14–19.

Garrett, George P. "Daily Life in City, Town, and Country." In Andrews, 1985, 215–32.

Gerard, John. 1951. *The Autobiography of an Elizabethan,* translated by Philip Caraman. London: Longmans.

Gerard, John. [1597] 1974. *The Herball: Or, Generall Historie Of Plants.* Norwood, NJ: Johnson.

Goodfellow, Peter. 1983. *Shakespeare's Birds.* Harmondsworth: Kestrel Books.

Grafton, Anthony. "Education and Apprenticeship." In Andrews, 1985, 55–65.

Greenblatt, Stephen J. 1973. *Sir Walter Ralegh: The Renaissance Man and His Roles.* New Haven: Yale University Press.

Greene, Graham. Introduction to *The Autobiography of an Elizabethan.* In Gerard, 1951, vii–xi.

Griffin, C. W. 1989. "Teaching Shakespeare on Video." *English Journal* 78.7: 40–43.

Grun, Bernard. 1975. *The Timetables of History.* New York: Simon.

Gurr, Andrew. 1987. *Playgoing in Shakespeare's London.* Cambridge, England: Cambridge University Press.

Hammersmith, James. 1990. "Theatre-in-the-Mind *Macbeth.*" East Alabama Regional In-Service Center. Auburn, February 13.

Hankins, John E., ed. *Romeo and Juliet.* In Harbage, 1969, 855–99.

Harbage, Alfred. 1966. *Conceptions of Shakespeare.* Cambridge: Harvard University Press.

————, ed. 1969. *The Complete Works of William Shakespeare.* Baltimore: Pelican.

————. 1970. *Shakespeare's Songs.* Philadelphia: Macrae Smith.

Harrison, G. B. 1955. *The Elizabethan Journals.* 3 volumes. Ann Arbor: University of Michigan Press.

Hawkes, Terence. 1985. "Telmah." In Parker and Hartman, 1985, 310–32.

Hayhoe, Mike. 1989. "Drama as Gaming: 'To Bestir and Busily Occupy.'" *English Journal* 78.4: 54–58.

"Hebrew Bible Sold for $3.19 Million." 1989. *The Washington Post* 113.1 (December 6): D14.

Heilbrun, Carolyn. 1957. "The Character of Hamlet's Mother." *Shakespeare Quarterly* 8: 201–06.

Heinig, Ruth Beall. 1988. *Creative Drama for the Classroom Teacher.* 3rd ed. Englewood Cliffs, NJ: Prentice-Hall.

Heninger, S. K., Jr. "The Literate Culture of Shakespeare's Audience." In Andrews, 1985, 159–74.

Hibbert, Christopher. 1971. *Tower of London.* New York: Newsweek.

Hindley, Geoffrey. 1979. *England in the Age of Caxton.* London: Granada.

Hirst, Derek. 1986. *Authority and Conflict: England 1603–1658.* London: Edward Arnold.

Hodges, C. Walter. 1949. *Shakespeare and the Players.* New York: Coward.

————. 1970. *Shakespeare and the Players.* London: Bell.

————. 1973. *The Globe Restored: A Study of the Elizabethan Theatre.* New York: Norton.

————. 1980. *The Battlement Garden.* New York: Houghton.

Hodges, C. Walter, S. Schoenbaum, and Leonard Leone, eds. 1979. *The Third Globe.* Detroit: Wayne State University Press.

Huggett, Richard. 1981. *The Curse of* Macbeth. Chippenham, Wiltshire: Picton.

Hummelen, W.M.H. "Types and Methods of the Dutch Rhetoricians' Theatre," translated by H. S. Lake. In Hodges, Schoenbaum, and Leone, 1979, 161–89.

Huntley, Frank L. 1964. "*Macbeth* and the Background of Jesuitical Equivocation." *PMLA* 79: 390–400.

Hussey, Maurice. 1978. *The World of Shakespeare and His Contemporaries: A Visual Approach.* London: Heinemann.

"James, Henry." In Campbell and Quinn, 1966, 395–96.

"Jonson, Ben." In Campbell and Quinn, 1966, 406–08.

Judges, Arthur Valentine, ed. 1930. *The Elizabethan Underworld: A Collection of Tudor and Early Stuart Tracts and Ballads Telling of the Lives and*

Misdoings of Vagabonds, Thieves, Rogues and Cozeners, and Giving Some Account of the Operation of the Criminal Law. New York: Dutton.

Kellogg, John B. 1988. "Forces of Change." *Phi Delta Kappan* 70: 199–204.

Kott, Jan. 1964. *Shakespeare Our Contemporary,* translated by Boleslaw Taborski. New York: Norton.

Kozintsev, Grigori. 1966. *Shakespeare: Time and Conscience,* translated by Joyce Vining. New York: Hill.

Levi, Peter. 1988. *The Life and Times of William Shakespeare.* London: Macmillan.

Levin, Harry. Introduction to *Coriolanus.* In Harbage, 1969, 1212–14.

Levine, Joseph M., comp. 1969. *Elizabeth I.* Englewood Cliffs, NJ: Prentice-Hall.

Levine, Lawrence. 1988. *Highbrow/Lowbrow: The Emergence of Cultural Hierarchy in America.* Cambridge: Harvard University Press.

Liu, Alan. 1989. "The Power of Formalism: The New Historicism." *English Literary History* 56: 721–71.

Lynn, Steven. 1990. "A Passage into Critical Theory." *College English* 52: 258–71.

Mallick, David. 1984. *How Tall Is This Ghost, John?* Adelaide: Australian Association for the Teaching of English.

Malloch, A. E. 1966. "Some Notes on Equivocation." *PMLA* 81: 145–46.

Martin, Colin, and Geoffrey Parker. 1988. *The Spanish Armada.* New York: Norton.

McManaway, James G. 1962. *The Authorship of Shakespeare.* Washington: Folger Shakespeare Library.

Miller, Edwin Haviland. 1959. *The Professional Writer in Elizabethan England: A Study of Nondramatic Literature.* Cambridge: Harvard University Press.

Milward, Peter, S.J. 1987. *Biblical Influences in Shakespeare's Great Tragedies.* Bloomington: Indiana University Press.

Morrill, John. 1984. "The Stuarts (1603–1688)." In *The Oxford Illustrated History of Britain,* edited by Kenneth O. Morgan, 286–351. Oxford: Oxford University Press.

Murphy, Peter E. 1984. "Poems and Poetry: Writing Useful for Teaching Shakespeare." *Shakespeare Quarterly* 35: 647–52.

Nicoll, Allardyce. 1957. *The Elizabethans.* Cambridge, England: Cambridge University Press.

Nuttall, A. D. 1983. *A New Mimesis: Shakespeare and the Representation of Reality.* London: Methuen.

Ong, Walter J. 1971. *Rhetoric, Romance, and Technology.* Ithaca: Cornell University Press.

————. 1982. *Orality and Literacy.* New York: Methuen.

Paolucci, Anne. "Shakespeare as a World Figure." In Andrews, 1985, 663–80.

Papp, Joseph. 1988. Foreword to *Macbeth.* In Bevington, vii–xv.

Parker, Patricia, and Geoffrey Hartman, eds. 1985. *Shakespeare and the Question of Theory.* New York: Methuen.

Partridge, Eric. 1968. *Shakespeare's Bawdy.* London: Routledge.

Patterson, Annabel. 1988. " 'The Very Age and Body of the Time His Form and Pressure.' " In *Shakespeare and Deconstruction,* edited by G. Douglas Atkins and David M. Bergeron, 47–68. New York: Lang.

Pease, Donald E. 1990. "Author." In *Critical Terms for Literary Study,* edited by Frank Lentricchia and Thomas McLaughlin, 105–17. Chicago: University of Chicago Press.

Pollard, Alfred W. [1917] 1937. *Shakespeare's Fight with the Pirates.* Cambridge, England: Cambridge University Press.

Pope, Elizabeth Marie. 1974. *Perilous Gard.* Boston: Houghton.

Pringle, Roger. "Sports and Recreations." In Andrews, 1985, 269–80.

"Prynne, William." In Campbell and Quinn, 1966, 662–63.

Reed, Arthea J. S. 1988. *A Teacher's Guide to the Signet Classic Edition of William Shakespeare's "Romeo and Juliet."* New York: New American Library.

Robinson, Randal. 1988. *Unlocking Shakespeare's Language.* Urbana: NCTE.

Ronayne, John. "Decorative and Mechanical Effects Relevant to the Theatre of Shakespeare." In Hodges, Schoenbaum, and Leone, 1979, 190–221.

Rosenfeld, Judith B. 1987. "An Elizabethan Interlude: A Course for Middle Schoolers." *English Journal* 76.8: 49–51.

Ross, Kathleen. 1989. "Bringing the Humanities to the Lower Achiever." *English Journal* 78.7: 47–48.

Ryane, Melody. 1990. Audience Question/Answer Session after *Major Barbara,* Alabama Shakespeare Festival, May 6.

Sargent, Ralph M., ed. *As You Like It.* In Harbage, 1969, 243–73.

Scher, Anna, and Charles Verrall. 1975. *100+ Ideas for Drama.* London: Heinemann.

Schoenbaum, S. 1977. *William Shakespeare: A Compact Documentary Life.* New York: Oxford University Press.

————. 1979. *Shakespeare, the Globe, and the World.* New York: Oxford University Press.

Seward, Desmond. 1983. *Richard III, England's Black Legend.* New York: F. Watts.

Showalter, Elaine. "Representing Ophelia: Women, Madness, and the Responsibilities of Feminist Criticism." In Parker and Hartman, 1985, 77–94.

Simmons, John S. 1968. "Shakespeare in the Boondocks." *English Journal* 57.7: 972–76.

Simon, John. "Shakespeare and the Modern Critic." In Andrews, 1985, 867–71.

Slavin, Arthur J. "Printing and Publishing in the Tudor Age." In Andrews, 1985, 129–42.

Smith, Lacey Baldwin. 1967. *The Horizon Book of the Elizabethan World.* New York: American Heritage Publishing Company.

———. 1975. *Elizabeth Tudor: Portrait of a Queen.* Boston: Little.

Sorlien, Robert Parker, ed. 1976. *The Diary of John Manningham of the Middle Temple 1602–1603.* Hanover, NH: University Press of New England.

Speaight, Robert. 1973. *Shakespeare on the Stage.* London: Collins.

Steiner, George. 1989. *Real Presences.* Chicago: University of Chicago Press.

Stone, Lawrence. 1967. *The Crisis of the Aristocracy, 1558–1641.* Abridg. ed. London: Oxford University Press.

Sutherland, James. 1970. "How the Characters Talk." In Cole, 1970, 76–84.

Tannahill, Reay. 1973. *Food in History.* New York: Stein.

Terwilliger, Robert E. 1981. "Politics and Christian Perception." In *Politics, Power, and Shakespeare,* edited by Frances McNeely Leonard, 69–71. Arlington: University of Texas at Arlington Press.

Thompson, Craig R. 1962. "Universities in Tudor England." In *Life and Letters in Tudor and Stuart England,* edited by Louis B. Wright and Virginia A. Lamar, 335–82. Ithaca: Cornell University Press.

Thomson, Elizabeth McClure, ed. 1965. *The Chamberlain Letters.* New York: Putnam's.

Thurber, James. 1988. "The *Macbeth* Murder Mystery." In *Shakespeare Merriment: An Anthology of Shakespearean Humour,* edited by Marilyn Schoenbaum, 169–74. New York: Garland.

Trevor-Roper, Hugh. 1981. Foreword to *The Lisle Letters.* In Byrne, 1981, ix–xiv.

Turberville, George. 1575. *The Booke of Faulconrie or Hawking.* London.

Vargas, Marjorie Fink. 1984. "Studying Nonverbal Communication through Creative Dramatics." *English Journal* 73.6: 84–85.

Veidemanis, Gladys. 1964. "Shakespeare in the High School Classroom." *English Journal* 53.4: 240–47.

Walizer, Marue E. 1987. "Adolescent Experience as Shakespearean Drama." *English Journal* 76.2: 41–43.

Warner, James A., and Margaret J. White. 1987. *Shakespeare's Flowers.* Wilmington, Del.: Middle Atlantic Press.

Weimann, Robert. 1978. *Shakespeare and the Popular Tradition in the Theatre.* Edited by Robert Schwartz. Baltimore: Johns Hopkins University Press.

———. "Mimesis in *Hamlet*." In Parker and Hartman, 1985, 275–91.

Wells, Henry W. [1924] 1961. *Poetic Imagery: Illustrated from Elizabethan Literature.* New York: Russell.

Wells, Stanley. 1984. *Re-editing Shakespeare for the Modern Reader.* New York: Oxford University Press.

Weston, William. 1955. *The Autobiography of an Elizabethan,* translated by Philip Carman. London: Longmans.

Whitaker, Virgil. 1953. *Shakespeare's Use of Learning.* San Marino: Huntington.

White, Beatrice. 1967. *Cast of Ravens: The Strange Case of Sir Thomas Overbury.* New York: Braziller.

Williams, George Walton. 1985. *The Craft of Printing and the Publication of Shakespeare's Works.* Washington: Folger Shakespeare Library.

Williams, Neville. "The Tudors." In Fraser, 1975b, 166–211.

Winter, William [1911] 1969. *Shakespeare on the Stage: First Series.* New York: Blom.

Author

Mary Ann Rygiel is currently teaching ninth-grade English at Auburn High School, Auburn, Alabama. She has also taught seventh-, tenth-, and twelfth-grade English. She is certified in English, math, and social studies. She has published on the literary style of the nineteenth-century Russian mathematician Sofya Kovalevskaya's memoir of childhood and on the poetry of George Herbert and Gerard Manley Hopkins. She has also published articles on English education. Her research interests include the Elizabethans, the Jacobeans, and the Victorians and their literatures. She lives in Auburn with her husband and their sons, Stephen, age fifteen, and Robert, age twelve.